No Room For Failure

No Room For Failure

8 Proven Strategies for Immediate Success in New Home and Real Estate Sales

Dr. Debora Trimpe

Published by Game Changer Publishing

ISBN: 978-1-7365491-9-3

GC | **Game Changer**
PUBLISHING

www.PublishABestSellingBook.com

DEDICATION

I dedicate this book to all the salespeople who have taught me so much about what it takes to succeed in this industry. I also want to express my heartfelt thanks to my husband, my mom, and my brother for encouraging me to write this book and embark on this new chapter of my career. Without their love and continuing support, this would never have become a reality.

DOWNLOAD YOUR FREE GIFTS

Read This First

Just to say thanks for buying and reading my book, I would like to give you a 100% bonus gift for FREE, no strings attached!

To Download Now, Visit:
www.NoRoomForFailureBook.com/freegift

No Room For Failure

8 Proven Strategies for Immediate Success
in New Home and Real Estate Sales

Dr. Debora Trimpe

GC Game Changer PUBLISHING

www.PublishABestSellingBook.com

Table of Contents

Introduction

IF YOU ARE READING THIS BOOK, I suspect that you fall into at least one of three categories. You are either just starting your career in new home sales or figuring out the best way to sell. You might be an individual that has done well recently in home sales or real estate, but for some reason, which you haven't been able to figure out, your career has stalled as if you have lost your magic. Last, you are one of those over-achiever types who are always reading and developing your craft to the next level. I can assure you of one thing, no matter which category you find yourself in, this book has the answers for you; however, I make that statement with a disclaimer. It has the answers if you are willing to be brutally honest with yourself about your skillset and the habits you have adopted. If you are eager to follow everything written here without dismissing it and are willing to do the work to adopt and practice these principles in your everyday sales life, this book is for you.

The other issue I believe you are facing as you read this is that you have some questions about me and what I bring to the table that no one else does. That's a pretty valuable question to ask. I don't believe just anybody, either. So, let me tell you a little about my

1

background. I've spent almost 40 years in this industry, working from being a salesperson to owning and managing my own home building company. Over the years, I have had the opportunity to coach and develop over a thousand people. The people I have coached have been new home sales professionals, realtors, realtor teams, sales teams, sales managers, company owners, and remodelers. After working with all of these people, many told me that I should write a book. My response was always to ask them what I should write a book about and why anyone would be interested in what I had to say. Every one of them said the same thing, "You have information that will be valuable to whoever reads it. I can assure you all the information you've given me has been valuable and helped me attain the success I have experienced." That's what they said.

The other thing I've seen in this industry is that very few people who are writing and teaching today spend much time, if any, out in the real world. We all know that things in the real world change almost on an hourly basis, if not weekly, daily, or monthly; there are so many different things that happen. There are various ways in which we look at the world, and there are so many aspects that can change.

During my career, I've continued to stay out in the mainstream, working with people day after day in the environment they experience every day. All of my business clients have more and more challenges they deal with. Most of my clients spend more time working than spending time with their families. Watching people sacrifice with little reward fueled a fire within me. If people are going to work so hard to be so successful, I want to make sure that they're making money while doing it. I want to make sure that they're successful in everything they do, every day they show up for work. That's why this book became a reality. It's an opportunity for all of us to reassess what we do, to look at the profession that we're in, and work at it in a very different way. That's the goal of this book. When you finish reading this, I want you to have strategies to help you achieve the performance levels you want and deserve.

Every one of these eight steps outlined within has been proven to help anyone who has implemented them consistently achieve the success they desired within this industry. The steps are pretty easy to implement. Unlike other books on sales, it allows you to retain your personality, not become a sales robot spouting the same questions and statements that everyone else does. This book is a roadmap that you can read once or re-read to continue to be creative and innovative within your business. Whichever path you choose, I know that you CAN have the success you have always dreamed of.

CHAPTER ONE

Change Your Mind, Change Your Success

SO MANY TIMES, WHEN I'M working with coaching clients, I find that they're their own worst enemy. I have had them tell me, "Oh gosh, I just can't be successful because the clients I have aren't interested in what I have to offer." - "Oh, I can't sell any homes because the prices have gone up exponentially. This just isn't going to work." - "Wow! My customers do not like my price increases." - "Oh, nobody wants this home. It's been on the market too long." - "Gosh, people come to my open houses, and they won't talk to me. I can't get any information out of them." Do any of these comments sound familiar? No, I didn't bug your car; I just know that this is what happens to all of us. We all tend to get in our own way.

Let me tell you a little story that might give you a clearer idea of what I'm talking about. I'm going to change the name to protect this successful gentleman and instead call him "Marvin." So, I worked with Marvin when he told me he couldn't sell any homes because of his competitors next door. He insisted that they told people stories about how bad he was as a salesperson and how bad his builder was. I said, "Wow, really? Do you think that they're saying that? Did you hear a customer say so?" He replied, "Well, no one's saying that, but I can tell you, Deb, people park their car in front of the competitor's model next door. They go in, 45 minutes later, they come out. They never come over to my model to look at it. Don't you think that's weird? Don't you think they would surely want to look at every model home on the street if they were interested in buying a home? I mean, I think I would." I told him I would do the same thing, look at every model on the street if I were interested in buying one, but that doesn't mean his competitors were badmouthing him, and that's why nobody ever goes to his model. But he insisted, saying, "I'm sure it is. I'm sure. I'm sure they tell the prospects that my price per square foot is too high or that they have more features. I know it."

Then I said, "Okay, Marvin, I'll tell you what we'll do. We'll go ahead and get somebody to visit this competitor and see what's going on." And so we hired a shopping service. They visited the model. Not surprisingly, the competitor never said even one bad thing about Marvin or the builder he works for. He confessed that he believed that the competitor was badmouthing him because *he* would be doing just that, badmouthing his competitor. He said that his competitor's price per square foot was much higher than his or that the competitor charges too much for the homes. That's when I told him, "Marvin, you see, *you* are in your way. They're not keeping you from selling any homes. They're not keeping prospects from walking into your door. They're doing nothing to harm you. It's *you* that's hurting you."

Suppose we look at some of the places we stumble in business or life, even if it's because we get in our way. What often happens in a situation is we have a perception of what is occurring. The definition of perception is "a way of regarding, understanding, or interpreting something; a mental impression." In this regard, what we perceive starts to paint a whole picture for us. For example, if we walked into a room and I said, "Oh, everything in here is dirty." What do you think you would do? You would walk into that room, expecting everything to be dirty. Now, maybe nothing's messy, but you'd be looking for that. You'd see a speck of dust, and suddenly you'd be saying, "Yes, she was right. The room is dirty."

Now, if I told you instead that it is the cleanest room you'll ever see before walking into the room, guess what? You'll walk into that room, expecting cleanliness. You'll be looking at how the windows are polished. You'll be looking at everything. Same room, no difference in circumstance, but the perception you had, the thoughts you had before going in, absolutely colored how you saw things. That's what happens in the sales opportunity. We develop a perception of what is occurring.

Now, if you have been in the business for very long, I'm sure you've heard the age-old statement, "Don't ever curb qualify." What does that mean for those of you who don't know? It means don't watch that person drive up and base his capacity to "qualify" for your services on the way he is dressed. That would be a big mistake. I have seen firsthand on more than enough occasions that people who come in with ratty jeans and a ripped shirt can buy a million-dollar house. The person who walks in with a brand spanking new BMW, Louis Vuitton bag in hand, perfectly dressed? She can't afford anything. So, don't let your perceptions about people, how they dress, how they talk, how they act create a mindset for you. Our perception of the situation now creates the second step – that is, to jump off and make an assumption.

Let's say I see a man get out of an old car wearing a ripped shirt and ripped jeans. He walks into my office, and here I am, selling a half-million-dollar home. Looking at the person, my initial perception is, "Wow, he doesn't look like he can afford this." So now what happens? I make certain assumptions. Well, if he can't afford this, what is he doing here? If he can't afford this, why is he wasting my time? If he can't afford this, what is his goal walking in here? Are they shopping me for someone else? It all starts with our perception, our mental impression of the person. I begin to make assumptions. Now, none of those assumptions are necessarily right. For example, let's say this person was Warren Buffet. If you met Warren Buffet in the early days, he'd drive up to your model in an old car wearing old jeans and a tee-shirt. He can afford a million-dollar house, that's for sure, but you would never have thought that by looking at him. So, I'd have a perception of the situation, right? I see how this all looks to me, and I start to make assumptions.

And now we get to point number three. Those assumptions lead to choices. Let's go back to our example. Buyer comes up, ripped jeans, ripped shirt, old car. Our honest perception? They don't look like they have much money. They walk into my office. The assumptions? They can't afford this. What are they here for? Are they scoping out my model home to come back and steal something later? Are they shopping me for somebody else? Are they just wasting my time? Are they just trying to get decorating ideas that they can't afford? Right? I start making choices on how to act based on those perceptions and assumptions. My choice is that I'm not going to waste my time with them. The action then is maybe I would speak rudely to them, or I decided to brush them off. Can you see how I can take a very qualified prospect and put them in a position where they would opt not to buy anything from me because of how I treated them?

Let's take another example. These prospects drive up in a shiny and expensive new car. In this scenario, the perception might be that they can afford my product. Then I start to make certain assumptions. Well, I don't need to determine if they are qualified for a home because I'm sure they can afford it. Look at what they're driving. I don't need to explain how much the monthly payment is because they probably already know that. I probably don't have to explain a lot about the quality and value. They have an expensive car, they have expensive clothes, and they probably understand the quality. So now, what do I do? I make choices about what I discuss and don't discuss with these buyers. Here are some of the actions I might take. I don't ask about the budget. I don't ask about where they want to be in a monthly payment range. I don't ask what's important to them in quality. I don't ask many great questions; I don't even try to figure out if I'm the right solution for them. As a result, what happens? Maybe I wasted hours with the wrong person, where I could have spent those same hours with the right one. Can you see how our mindset gets in our way just by curb qualifying traffic?

Let's go to another problem that people face: "My prices are too high." Oh gosh, that's always fun. "My prices are too high." - "My customers all think my prices are too high." Let me tell you about a scenario where these perceptions, assumptions, and choices affected another person I was coaching. We will call her Sandy. Sandy told me, "You know, my customers can't believe how much my prices have gone up." She had been in this particular neighborhood with this builder for five years; she was the first salesperson out there. She knew what prices were five years ago. She continued to watch prices go up. Often, her prices go up and then down to an affordable price and then up again. Sandy was overly consumed by her price structure, so I asked her, "How many people have you worked with for two to three years who are shocked at how much your prices have gone up?"

"Well, no one," she replied. So how did her customers know that her prices had gone up? She had no answer because she was never able to tell them that her prices went up. These new customers had no idea. It was her mindset. It was her perception that she wasn't selling homes because her prices had gone up too much. She assumed that this wouldn't be something people would want to buy because they would think it was too expensive and did not have enough included features. As a result, she treated every prospect she had as probably not a buyer because she believed they wouldn't buy anyway.

Let me share another example with you. Melvin worked in a close-out neighborhood. His builder built some inventory homes for him, but they were four homes all of the same floor plan. Melvin called me complaining about the fact that these homes were all the same. He also explained he wouldn't sell them because his buyer demographics weren't matching these one-story homes. They wanted big two-story homes with five bedrooms, not one-story homes with three bedrooms and a study. Melvin wanted me to agree with him that he had a monumental problem that just wasn't going to allow him to sell homes. His perception was that he had a product that no one would buy because that was not what his customers were asking for. He assumed that he would go broke because there was no market for what he had.

His choice was to complain and quit trying to sell these homes. Unfortunately, or maybe, fortunately, Melvin did not get the response he was hoping for from me. He was hoping I would agree. As you might guess, I did not. I told Melvin that while the typical buyer he saw might not want to buy that type of home, there would still be buyers who would. I asked him to define the perfect buyer for those homes. After about five minutes, we found four different buyer profiles that would find that these homes are exactly what they wanted. Currently, these types of buyers were not coming in to see Melvin. We began to discuss different marketing tactics we could utilize to find these buyers and bring them in. When we were finished, we had over a dozen other tactics Melvin agreed he would use. The results? Within two weeks from launching his plan, he sold two of the four homes and had prospects coming in to see the remaining two.

The reason Melvin wasn't selling those homes was not that there were no buyers; Melvin wasn't selling homes because he had gotten in his own way. He had the wrong mindset. He was focused on the way things had been, not on how they could be. He was mired in self-pity and hopelessness. The minute he changed his perception about these homes, his assumptions changed. And once his assumptions had changed, his choices changed. Once his choices had changed, his results changed. It is that simple.

Suppose you're struggling with your sales and your production. In that case, even if you're struggling with something you're trying to accomplish in your business, I might suggest you look at your mindset because so often, that is what's holding you back. Once you change your outlook on the situation, once you change your perception, change your assumptions, then the actions you choose to take will change as well; so will your results.

ACTION PLAN:

- After reading through this first chapter, try as much as you can to be introspective. Write down all of the reasons why you think you're not as successful as you'd like to be. That would be very helpful because by doing that, you will be able to identify what's keeping you from your goal. Then you can reevaluate why you feel that way.

- Once you've identified all the things that keep you from being successful, go back and review each situation or issue. Based on your problems, what are the perceptions that we can draw from there as a result? What assumptions are you making? And last, what actions are you doing now that is maybe undermining your success?

- When you have an interaction, slow it down. If you'll stop and catch yourself before you start with these perceptions, then move on to assumptions and avoid taking the wrong action, you will probably see that you're either on the right track or the wrong track and save yourself a lot of time and a lot of heartbreak. Remember, slow everything down.

CHAPTER TWO

Without Leads, You Have No Chance

SO MANY PEOPLE WANT TO KNOW, how do I get more leads? You know, I want to step back one moment before we go into lead generation here and tell you, as you'll learn in the rest of this book, it's what you do with the lead that matters the most, not how many leads you get. I've learned from coaching people all these years because people always want more leads or more traffic because they don't have to work so hard at converting. You only really need one qualified person to buy anything from you. You don't have to have 15; you don't have to have 20. Sometimes you only just need one. That being said, if you don't have the one, life is kind of tough. I'll use an example here.

As you can see by this book's date, it is written pretty much during the fun of the COVID-19-coronavirus we've experienced here in the United States. I would like to tell you the story of Sarah. Sarah started with this home builder in a brand-new position as a salesperson. She began in March of 2020. Sarah lived in Texas, and when the virus hit, the Texas Governor ordered everyone to stay home. Fortunately for us in the real estate business, we were deemed an essential service. Therefore, we could go to work. Unfortunately for Sarah, though, she was brand new to this community and had no one to follow up with. She had no leads; she had zero. At this point, people weren't coming to open houses. People weren't walking into every model home checking things out. Traffic prospects had pretty much died to almost nothing. When we started working together, Sarah had no leads. Imagine no one walked in the door for four weeks from when she got into that neighborhood.

Now we had to work pretty hard and fast trying to generate traffic for her, and we did. She went from zero to 20 sales in just four months during a pandemic! Go figure, right? You ask, how do we create leads? Because if we don't have leads, we don't have a prospect to work with. There's no way we can make a sale.

What we found successful is what I will just call the **three-bucket system**. At one point in time back when the great recession was in place, starting around 2008, we used to call this three-bucket system the "recession-proof marketing plan." It focuses on three basic things to obtain traffic. One is referrals. You know that referrals are probably the best opportunity for getting leads for most people. If you're able to figure out how to get referrals, you're set for life. Two, working with clients who have common interests with you, and number three is self-generating your own traffic from the world around you. So, let's deep dive into this and see what we can come up with.

Let's talk about referrals first. We know we can get referrals from past customers, right? But how many of you work with past customers? Here's where my readership will pretty much divide: New home sales and realtors. Many of you are in new home sales, and as a new home salesperson, you make a sale, and you are pretty much one and done. What do I mean by that? You get a prospect, they come in, they buy a house, you get them moved into that house, and you move on and forget they ever existed.

The realtors who are reading this book look at the world in a very different way. Every person you work with is a future lister. Referrals are an absolute repository of great potential leads; it doesn't matter if you're the new home salesperson or the realtor. This is the way I see it.

Most people are not working very effectively or efficiently. So how do I get past customers to refer people to me? Well, first of all, whether you are a new home salesperson or a realtor, you can all do this. If you think about it, it's safe to say that we all know about 200 to 250 people, but we may not be very close to each one of them. Do you get me? I mean, you might have heard the saying Six Degrees of Separation from Kevin Bacon. The idea is that if you talk to six people, you'll get to know somebody that knows somebody that knows Kevin Bacon, the actor. We know a lot of people. We know we're not all best friends. We don't have lunch with them every day or go out to movies with them, but we know people from work or our kids' schools or church. We know them from a soccer team, baseball team, football team, neighbors, there are all sorts of people we know. So, the first step I want you all to take, no matter which side of selling you're on, is to take five of those names every day and commit to writing a note to them, telling them that you are selling homes. Don't assume that just because you told somebody five years ago that you are in real estate sales that they remember that today. People need to be reminded, so take the step, present that personal touch, handwrite something, and send it. I would even suggest using regular old snail mail. It still works! In fact, snail mail gets a lot of attention because few use it anymore.

If you get a card with a handwritten address on it, how many of you still open it? We all do, I bet. Even when we think it's computer-generated, we always open it because we believe somebody sent us something. Why? Because sometimes people actually still send us birthday cards, and it's nice to send back little thank you notes. We look forward to many things in the mail, besides all of the bills we get and all of the little ads for everything you can imagine possible. So that's number one. Number two is we've got to ask for a referral every time we interact with a past customer. Here's where I see most people fall down. I'll ask them, did you ask that person about a referral? "Oh gosh, no, I forgot." Or I get somebody who says, "Well, gosh, if I ask them every time, they know I'm going to ask for a referral." So, there's the point. It's okay for them to know that you're probably going to ask for a referral every time. It's okay to ask frequently because life gets in the way. So, don't be surprised if they don't get back to you. It's not because they don't like you or don't want to help you. It's just that they had more important things to do than worry about your business.

Number two, how we ask customers is also our downfall. As I just mentioned before, we have approximately 250 people that we know. So, if you say to me, "Hey, who do you know that's looking to buy a home?" All of a sudden, these 250 names start sorting through the file cabinet in my brain. As soon as I get through about six or seven names, I'm already worn out. And that's why you get the answer, "Let me think about it and get back to you," because I'm already overwhelmed at the question. So, what I'd like them to do is take that number of 250 people they know and reduce that down into subsets of people. That way, it's easier to go through that mental file cabinet.

Here's what I mean by that. I will ask, "Hey, who do you know at church…" if they attend or work at a church. All of a sudden, instead of thinking about 250 names, they might be thinking about 10, 15, or 20 people they know from the church; there's the subset of names I'm talking about. The same thing might apply to a customer who is very involved in their kid's soccer league. Maybe the next time they call you and say, "Hey, who do you know in your kid's soccer league that mentioned they were thinking about moving?" Of course, I'm going through the parents in the soccer league, not all 250 people I know in the file cabinet, but maybe only 20 or 25. When you ask about a referral from a subset, you make it so much easier for that person to drill down to someone they can refer to.

The next crucial point is how you ask for the referral. Here's what I mean by that. If you'll notice, what I said to them is who do they know that has mentioned they're thinking of moving. This is the key phrase, "Who is thinking of moving." Use phrases that people most often use to help somebody remember a conversation. For example, if I'm in new home sales and I said, "Who do you know who is looking for a new home?" Let's face it. If I'm standing at the microwave in the kitchen at work, I'm not probably sitting there thinking I might want to buy a new home this week. So what would I say to my co-workers? I might say something like, "Gosh, our house is getting too small. We're thinking about moving." That's where it starts. If you use a phrase that they would have heard someone else use, it is a trigger. It's a trigger to remember that conversation.

If you're a realtor, think about it. Many people say, "You know, we're thinking about putting our house on the market." They don't say, "We think we're going to list our home with a realtor." So, I wouldn't say to somebody, "Who do you know at your kid's school that has said they are thinking about listing their home with a realtor?" People don't talk that way. It's preferable to ask, "Who do you know at your kid's school who's mentioned that they wanted to put their house on the market." That's what they usually say. And when you use these triggers, it is so much easier to remember a person. You'll be surprised at how many more names you'll get more frequently.

Now, another target we're looking at in this referral situation is current customers. Many people have said you should go ahead and start asking people for the referral as soon as you sign a contract; I disagree. I don't think that you can ask anybody for a referral when you've just written a contract. Why? Because they have no idea what level of service you're going to offer. Think about it, a referral is really about the service that they thought you offered. Think about it in this way. When you go to Amazon to buy something from a seller you've never seen before, what do you do? You go to the star ratings, and you look for what people said about the product or the service, right?

If you're a realtor, they need a real relationship with you to say this service was excellent. Same thing if you sell for a builder. If the customer had just barely talked to you, they don't know about the quality of the product or service that you are giving them. So, when you ask current customers, wait until they've seen some level of service from you. This doesn't mean you have to wait until they close but wait until they've developed enough trust and have seen you work your magic for them so they might feel they would want to refer someone.

Here's the third part that's really important about referrals. Myers Barnes, a fabulous sales trainer, talks about referrals in this way. He says, "You know, when you ask someone to give a referral, you're actually asking that person if you can borrow their reputation." Wow, that's very powerful to consider it that way. When you talk with that referral, you are saying, "Your friend said I should call you because they had a great experience." So always think about that. Suppose the person you ask for a referral has had no level of service interaction with you. Why would they allow you to use their reputation to get another prospect?

Another thing you should think about with referrals is it's always better to give than to receive. I heard that all my life and many people tell me, "Deb, that's not really helpful." Oh, but it is. Think about it this way. What can I give somebody that might motivate them to provide me with something in return? For my builder friends, what you might want to consider is to do something as simple as a monthly email to all of your buyers who moved into homes, giving them some kind of warranty information about the care of their homes. So, what do I mean by that? You might say, "Hi guys, it's April. You realize that you should replace your air filter for your HVAC system at least every couple of months? It's spring. You're doing spring cleaning. Don't forget to change your filters." That's a nice little note or a reminder. It might be a reminder about when to change their timing on their sprinkler systems. Is that something that you do? The same thing for my realtor friends, it's a great idea to tell people Spring is a good time to change filters. Or think about what your landscape has to do with how people perceive the exterior of your home, so you might want to refresh your landscaping. You can develop your own list, where you have a different idea for every month. Send out that email, and then, at the bottom of that email, you should always ask for a referral. So, do you see what I'm saying? I'm going to give them something, a little nugget on how to care for their home and in return, I'm going to ask them for a referral.

This is an idea for my realtor friends. Every year when assessed values are out, many realtors will send out a note confirming that values have come out from the taxing authority. You could send a note to customers asking, "If you'd like me to look at comps in your area to see if your assessed value is too high, let me know, I can help you. Give me a call. By the way, do you know anyone who said they were thinking about putting their home on the market?

I'd love to give them the same service I've given you." But again, if I want to get something, offer up something that would be a value to them first before asking in return. And then, as I said before, just remember to ask with every interaction. Once you have earned trust with people, once they see the service level you have to offer, every time you interact with them, ask for the referral.

Now let's talk about our second step in trying to always create leads. And that is work with someone with like clients. So, what does that mean? Let's talk about all of you that may sell homes for a builder. Who has clients? Hmm.

The first one that will pop up for any of you who've done this for any length of time is realtors. Realtors are always working with buyers who are looking for homes, right? So that's a perfect connection. Now what I'm going to say to you is to go ahead and ask these realtors to bring their prospects to you when they don't know you; why would they do that? I am always here. I have a home. You have a buyer. Why can't we mix the two together? Well, what I know is most people do business with people they like, trust, and respect. Now that like, and trust doesn't end up with me asking you for business. It may start with me telling you how I can bring business to you. Okay. So, my builder friends, you're going to be working with my realtor friends and my realtors. You're going to be trying to work with builders, right?

Builders have people come in every day, and a lot of them have homes to sell. Some of them have realtors already, but if not, the salesperson can refer that person who doesn't have a realtor to you. How do you get on that list? How do you become one of the people that they refer to, right? This is where it becomes critically important to remember to consider what you can do for the other person whose business you want to get.

So, for my builder friends, what does a realtor want? They want clients. If I'm going to go out and reach out to realtors, I will not tell realtors what product I have to sell, begging them to sell it for me. I'm going to go search out realtors that I believe would be good at helping prospects who walk into my office who really need help. Maybe they have a home to sell. Maybe they're in the wrong price point altogether. I just feel bad for anybody bumping around in today's world, trying to find a home on their own. There are so many different resources. It's so dang confusing. I'd want them to work with a reputable realtor to find a house, even if it's not in my price range.

So, builders, your call and your conversation needs to be with realtors about how do I bring you the right kind of buyers that you can work with or the right people that have listings? What does your best customer look like?

Realtors, let's take the flip side here. What do you offer a builder? Many of you, my realtor friends, have awesome social media presences, better than my builder friends do.

Maybe it's a way to teach them about social media. Maybe it's a way to help them post on social media. Maybe it's a way to post their neighborhood on your social media site and promote that builder or promote that location or promote that specific model. Maybe they're a small builder who really could use your help by having an open house in one of their inventory homes if they have one, so they can bring in additional traffic. Again, how do you bring service to them? You're not going to say to them, "I need buyers. I need people that want to list their house. Who do you have?" They're just going to say to you as the realtor, "Who are you going to bring to me to buy a home?" It's always about how do you help one another?

Another option might be insurance agents. In most areas, insurance agents are always stopping off at realtor offices, always stopping off in builder offices, trying to promote their insurance because obviously, when somebody buys a home, they need insurance. And a lot of times, that's when someone will actually think about shopping for their insurance. When you have a home that you've been in for years, you don't think about shopping around or trying to get a better rate. It just seems too difficult. When you're buying a new home, you start thinking maybe I could get it cheaper. Maybe I could get better service. So, what about working with local insurance agents, talking to them about what their best customer looks like, and how can you all work together to bring more buyers in for you? Obviously, they have people that call them all the time. What if one of their customers calls and says, "We have to replace the roof on our house. We've been in our house for 20 years. We're starting to think maybe we should move." Why is that person not referring you business? There's an opportunity.

Another possibility we want to talk about is mortgage lenders. Now, many of you builders have your own in-house lenders that you work with. I also know that some deals just can't be made with an in-house lender. At that point in time, you'll work with somebody else. So, my question is, with all these lenders who want business, who are they going to bring to you?

If somebody comes to get pre-qualified, my first question would be, "Where are you looking at buying a home? You should look over here. You should look at what my friend, Suzy, can do for you." Same thing with you, realtors, you get a lender that you work with, and you send most of your business to them. What business are they bringing back to you in today's world? The best way for all of us to be successful is to work together, to bring business to everyone. I want to bring business to someone who's going to bring it back to me, not just be bringing business to someone who will never reciprocate. So that's our section on working with someone with like clients.

Our third piece is self-generating your traffic from the world around you. What does that mean? That seems awfully difficult. It's really not. It just requires some creativity. And for those of you who are reading this saying, "Oh, I'm not creative," let's talk about some ideas. This works for both my realtor friends and my home builder friends. What about a local gym? I'm not talking about the major chains, but there are a lot of local gyms that have popped up along the way. I know workout classes have become really popular for women in my area, and yoga has taken off. What about if I went to that yoga studio and I went to the owner of the yoga studio and said to her, "What can we do to work together? You have lots of people that come in here taking yoga classes. They obviously are from the area. Some of them are looking for a home. What can we do to reciprocate?" If I'm a builder, I might say, "I'll tell you what, Carrie, I could put the good word out there about your gym, and maybe in return, you could do the same for me?" "If anyone you refer comes into my sales office, and they buy a home from me, I will come back, and I will pay for six months of their membership at your yoga studio." Wow, that's helpful for everybody. Carrie sends somebody who's already in the neighborhood to you. They buy a house from you. You make sure they keep going to her yoga studio for the next six months.

What about restaurants? You know, when the pandemic erupted, it changed so many things, and I believe it will forever change how people eat out. We've now learned that curbside delivery is really something to think about that. It used to be called carry out. Now it's curbside delivery. The person from the restaurant delivers it to you in your car, and you take it home. You're the delivery person, right? What about going to the local restaurant as a realtor and saying to them, "I'll tell you what, if you will put my flyer on every carry-out bag you take out, or every delivery you take out if a person gives me that flyer and they buy home with me, as a closing gift I will buy a hundred-dollar gift card for them at your restaurant." They get a continued patron. You get a customer. Think about that.

I had a client years ago that went to a local pizzeria, and they brought their flyer in. They were in a first-time homebuyer market, and they brought their flyer into the pizzeria, asked if they would go ahead and put their flyer on the top of the pizza box because guess what? There were lots of apartments that surrounded this particular place, and who eats out a lot? A lot of apartment dwellers eat pizza. So, they started doing that, and this particular builder saw a big influx of traffic and made multiple sales off of just that simple thing about putting their flyer on the top of a pizza box. Who would have thought, right? But it has to go to the right market. What about doing something like this?

What about doing a service for both your buyer and the business? I have some friends who have gone out and created a book of business, we call it. What they do is they go to the different businesses around and say, "Look, I have a group of new buyers that are coming into this area, coming in to buy homes for me, moving into my neighborhood. And they always ask the same questions. Things like 'where's the closest dry cleaner, where can I get my haircut? Is there an office supply store near here? Where can I get something printed?' And so, I'm creating a book that I'm giving all of my customers at closing so that they know more about the neighborhood. Now, the only people I'm putting in this book are people that are helping me.

So how might you be able to market me and my services in your establishment, knowing that I'm going to continue to market your establishment to everyone that closes on a home with me?" And that has worked really, really well for the friends of mine that have done that. They have created great relationships with local business people. When people walk into a place to do business, it's amazing the things they start talking about. In fact, I would try to get to know the local barber and certainly the local hairdresser, because if you're a woman, you know, that hairdresser probably knows more about your personal life than any other human being on the planet; just saying,

How about Toastmasters? I know this is a group that probably many of you have never even heard about. Joining Toastmasters is a great opportunity because, first of all, it's a group of people that teach you about speaking in public. Who wouldn't like to be a better public speaker? That's the number one fear people have, getting up in front of a group of people and speaking. So, you learn a great skill, and you hang out with like-minded people who are interested in developing themselves. They're surrounded by other business people who want to learn to speak in public for their own business. It's a great opportunity to network with other like-minded business professionals.

Another place to look for business is the chamber of commerce. Now I hate for any person from the chamber to read this book because they're not probably going to like what I say. I'm not sure I want to go to every ribbon cutting of every business that ever exists, but they do have networking sessions where they have other business people come into the network with other business professionals. That's the group I want to be. Part of that group are the people who I can help, and the other part of the group are the people who can help me.

Almost 40 years ago, when I started in the business, they had such a thing, and they are starting to make a resurgence yet again. Those are leads clubs. What I mean by a leads club is that it's a group of individuals who get together, eat at a local area restaurant, or maybe somewhere else, and they share leads. Usually, in a leads club, they will restrict how many people can belong to that particular club from a profession. So, if you're a new home salesperson or you're a realtor, you're not going to go to a leads group where there are 50 other realtors or new home salespeople. What you do is you go there, you meet a lot of other people, you bring them leads, they bring you leads.

For example, you are a new home salesperson, and you're working with the HR director of some company and someone else in the leads group sells copiers, maybe that's a lead that you can put together. They can call the HR department who's talked about adding more people, and if they're adding more people, they might need more copiers. And so, as you can see, it's an opportunity to start to share leads.

Another place would be physicians and nurse recruiters because hospitals are always looking for more physicians in today's world, and they're always looking for more nurses. Some hospitals recruit themselves, and some people actually use recruiters. How great is it to call up that recruiter and tell them you would be more than happy to give them information on the local area, information on schools, information on shopping, all these different things if they would consider at least sending out information on your company when they have people interested in the area? It's a great way for them to get the information they need to send out that might interest somebody in the area. Plus, sending your brochure along may be helpful because a lot of times, these physicians and nurses are also asking what's the cost of housing. If they move, they have to live somewhere. So, you are a benefit in that way as well.

What about working with HR departments? How would I work with an HR department? Well, think about this. Most companies would prefer that someone owns a home a short drive time from where they work. What they've learned is that when people have a job and live within a certain commute distance, they tend to stay at the same job longer. Because guess what? If I'm looking for a new job, I have to try to find a job in the same area. If not, I'm going to have to probably move because the commute is too long. This works, especially in big cities. So, this is really important to think about. HR departments want people to buy homes because it keeps them at their job. These days more and more people are starting to work more remotely, which is also helpful for us because now people are willing to look in more of what used to be undesirable locations further out in the suburbs, because they're not so worried about commute times. That being said, HR departments are always looking for great, informative ways to keep their employees educated. Who's educating them on real estate? Real estate is an important part of almost everybody's life. Most people aspire to own a home, and people who already own homes want to sell their homes. What have you created for these HR departments? Some kind of a lunch and learn where you put on a program, perhaps on how to buy a new home. Granted, you have to remember this can't be a sales pitch for you or you're out the door. They don't want a sales pitch, but we can provide really great third-party learning opportunities for these people. A lot of people have no idea if they're a first-time buyer or what it takes to buy a home. You can work with your lenders to talk about how you qualify for a home. You can talk about how you pick a listing agent? If you have a house to list, why is it important to pick the right listing agent, what is a current market analysis? How do you assess what a current market analysis is? How do you read it, how do you define it? How do you figure out if the realtor is telling you the truth? These are all different topics that you can expand upon, so figure out what your topic is. Figure out a presentation that could be held within 45 minutes of a lunch hour and provide lunch. Figure out if you're going to do it at their corporate campus or office. If not, if people are going to attend via a zoom meeting or some kind of other platform meeting where they don't come into the office. Perhaps you can go ahead and send everybody a $5 gift card in addition to the free lunch on you. Just be smart about it because there are lots of opportunities.

The last thing I want to talk to you about in lead generation and finding people to buy is do you have a marketing plan, and probably most important, do you follow it? For my realtor friends, I think everybody in real estate has now become a social media maven. Everybody talks about social media being the thing, right? Get a platform, get out there and get in front of people, it's not bad, it's good. I see social media as awesome for creating a brand for yourself. That being said, what are you actually doing to market the particular properties that you have? Obviously, some people do videos. Some people go ahead and take photos and put them out on their social space. But there are other marketing things, as we've just addressed that can be done that are really, really important and can drive even more qualified traffic.

Here's what happens when we have no traffic, just like my friend Sarah had zero people to work with. We get really, really, really dedicated to market, market, market. And then here's what happens.We start to sell. And then when we start to sell, what happens to marketing? It falls off. This is really true for my realtor friends too. What happens when you let that marketing plan fall off? All of a sudden, you see, I have no more leads to work. Now what do we do? Get really busy and start marketing. Unfortunately, marketing efforts take between four to six weeks to actually produce strong and consistent results. So, do you really want to have that gap in your production? Do you really want to have no closings for a month or two months? Make sure that you have a great plan. Your plan should be a monthly plan. You should be committed each month to what marketing activities you are going to undertake, and you need to make sure that it's a plan that you can stay up with. If you can't stay up with the plan, it will never work.

As I discussed before, social media isn't everything. Still, it is something most people expect today, which is to see you somewhere out there in the social media space. Now, the important part about that is, is make sure you're in the social media space that corresponds with the demographics of who you're selling homes to or that you're working with. If you're working with a lot of millennials, you might not find them on Facebook as much, but you might find them on Twitter or Instagram. If you're working with empty-nester buyers, you're not finding them on Twitter and Instagram. Still, you are finding them on Facebook because that's the only way they can keep up with their kids and grandkids. You get my drift?

Great marketing is also about differentiation. It isn't always about branding. And that's what I see so many people doing in their marketing plan. It's, "Who am I as a brand?" That's great, and I don't want to take anything away from that. In fact, one of my really successful realtor teams is doing eight figures in business, yes, eight figures, over a hundred million dollars in transactions last year. They have branding that is awesome. But one of the things that the founder of this company has done is she's figured out how to differentiate herself from the rest of the market. She differentiates herself in the way of telling personal stories about herself. She wants people to get to know who she is. She lets people in the inner sanctum, and the more they feel like they know about her, the more connected they feel to her, and the more likely they are to do business with her.

I am always working with teams on marketing activities. You know, for my realtors, it may be door knocking. It may be, "How do we make a great successful open house, our marketing effort this month?" And those people who have a great marketing plan, who do consistently large numbers in business, make their marketing plan a daily ritual. It is not an afterthought. It is part of their routine. Once you lose your way with your marketing plan, once you stop marketing, you lose your mojo. I can tell you once you let up, nobody's coming in the door. Once those numbers fall off, and you don't feel like there's a consistent number of people to work with, you lose your ability to sell. That's where I see so many people get down. I don't have any traffic to make a sale. What are we doing to market? Nothing, and that's the problem. We start to spiral down into this sad state of affairs, where we have no traffic. We have no sales, and it just keeps building on itself. What I can tell you is in this business, and you've probably heard this from many people before, activity breeds activity. Some of the activities you may engage in may not bring one traffic unit in your door and not one qualified lead. But interestingly enough, that activity of working on the marketing plan every day and all of the things you have to get done.It keeps your energy level up. And one of the things so many people tell me, "Oh, Deb, I know I'm really kind of down and out, but I got to tell you when somebody walks in that door, I am *on* like you wouldn't believe." No, you're not. When we let our activity and our energy levels die, that comes across to buyers in a negative way. When you're active and getting things done, people sense that about you. People sense that activity, the busy-ness, the purposefulness of what you do, and that's the kind of individual they want to buy from.

ACTION PLAN:

- You might take some of the ideas we talked about or maybe, on your own, create a list of three activities you are going to undertake to get referrals.

- List three activities you are going to engage in to get people and similar businesses to work with you.

- List three self-generation traffic activities you're going to engage in.

- Create your marketing plan and then continue that marketing plan every month for an entire year. That's not set in stone. You can go ahead and change that up but set the plan and start to work the plan today.

- The last thing I want to say about activities is to stop changing. I guarantee you that if I asked you who Jack in the Box is, you could all tell me about the ping pong ball-shaped head with the pointy hat who is the spokesperson for Jack in the Box restaurants. Have they changed that guy's look anytime in the last ten years? No. That's a reminder that you'll get tired of your marketing message because you see it all the time. Remember, your customer doesn't see your marketing message every time you send it out, so stop changing the message. Let the message stand. Let the message work.

CHAPTER THREE

The Dollars Are in the Demonstration

IN THE LAST CHAPTER, I talked about Sarah, a newbie home salesperson with zero track record who became a superstar selling sensation in just five months. Sarah sold nothing in the first month, but when the second month came she sold three! And this is out of a limited number of leads. Obviously, I asked her, "Why are you selling homes? What's the secret to your success? You know, you're working with limited numbers of people, and you seem to be converting almost everybody." And she said, "It's because I followed everything you told me to do with the demonstration. And I know that when I do what you taught me to, I get the answers I need from people. It's really, really easy to figure out what they need and how to put them in it. And so, getting clients into the right house and then going ahead and putting them on a contract is the simplest thing I've ever done." How many of you can really say that writing a deal is the simplest thing you've ever done? I will admit to you, this is the place I see most people struggle, and it's because no one really has helped.

For my real estate friends, there's nowhere in getting a license that requires you to learn anything about marketing or sales. Those of you who are my builder friends, there are many people out there teaching and selling. There's a lot of people who have written books about sales. Although there's not a lot of books about new home sales, there are many books about selling, which isn't always the same because buying a house is a very emotional experience compared to buying a product.

As I said before, many of the people who teach sales haven't spent a day in a sales office in quite some time. I started in this industry teaching salespeople how to sell back in the early eighties. What I taught then are things that I would never teach today. It would never work. The hard close doesn't work. Only showing them five houses doesn't work. Very educated people know so much more than we give them credit for and that has totally changed everything about this business.

The first thing I think all of us need to do is step back and realize that we have to understand what the buyer needs to know to decide. Somebody taught me this years ago, and I've kept it in my arsenal because it makes a lot of sense to me. Every buyer has questions. They need answers. Now I'm going to make this statement. It doesn't mean you're going to ask these questions in your presentation. And it doesn't mean that you're going to make a presentation that gives facts about these things. Many of us in sales are giving people information we think they need. I'm sorry, you don't live with them. You don't know what their problems really are. You weren't in the car with them in the middle of their argument on their way to the model home today. You have no idea what they just talked about on the phone or that their kids are having issues. We know nothing about that person. Yet, when they walk into our sales office or walk into our open house or call us on the phone about a listing, we start to create a perception (which we learned about earlier). We then make assumptions and then go into our plan of action. So, what are these questions?

Well, first of all, I think most of these people are going to know, "Why should I even buy a home?" However, that is a critical question for a first-time buyer. Why shouldn't they just keep leasing? Why don't they want to stay mobile? For those of our buyers who had owned homes before, it was kind of an easy one. "I can see the value of owning a home," they will say. But think about some of the buyers we start working with who are the empty nesters or the retirees. Is it best to buy another home? To own a home? Is it better to go into independent or assisted living? There are so many options out there. Usually, the first question they're trying to figure out is, "Should I even buy a home? Does this make sense for me?" Another question that they would have is, "Why would I want to buy from this person?" All of you have probably read books that say you have to build trust for people to buy from you.

It's interesting because they don't just have to trust the process, prospects first have to like you. Once they like you, they have to trust you. And once they actually trust you, they respect you. And when they get to the respect factor, that's when they finally buy.

So, what is it about you that makes you different from everybody else? What is it about you that they feel makes you likable? What is it about you that makes them think you're trustworthy? What do you know that someone else doesn't now? I'll tell you, there's a straightforward answer. The answer is to understand the buyer well enough to give them what they want, and you'll win every time.

A third question, which would be for my home builders especially is "Why would I want to buy from you versus the competition?" Now it works for my realtor friends as well, "Why would I want to buy this home versus the other homes out there listed on the market," right? That is the competition. So, let me talk to my builder friends for a moment when we're talking about why buy me versus the competition. This is about differentiation. It's about the little things that you do differently that make you unique. It is not about the big stuff. What little things do you want to hit on for those people? What little things do you want to talk about? The information you provide depends on the buyer. Don't go in with a preconceived set of notions. Also, understand your competition isn't always just another builder. It may be resale.

Many of my realtor friends don't even know what else they're looking at. Some of you see people and don't even have them sign a buyer's agent agreement with you. Often, you find out that they are working with two or three other realtors with no buyer's agent agreement signed. So, it's interesting how little we often know about what other people have looked at or what else they're considering that would be competition for the property you are showing them.

Another question is, "Why would I want to buy this particular house versus where I live now?" You know, one of the things that the coronavirus pandemic created is when you are stuck at home, you can easily recognize how small the room is, how insufficient the insulation is, how inefficient the energy is. My kids are all over me. You can name it once you've lived in a house and can't really go out and do much. You pretty much understand why that house doesn't fit. However, when life appears relatively normal, and people go around with all of their activities, like families being super involved in kids' sports and all these children's activities, some of these realizations are not as clear. I have parents who are seniors, and they're involved in church, they're involved in the senior center, they play bridge, they have a huge active lifestyle, actually more active than mine is. I just seem to work all the time. Now you may love what you do and feel like it'll never work, but when you can't get out of the house, you start to see some of these things as glaring that maybe you didn't really notice before. Maybe that's when you start to really consider a move.

But this usually brings on that secret pain, which is change. Whatever change they have to go through is going to be painful for someone. So, is the pain of change worth the benefit they think they're going to receive by buying this different house? It is our job to help them find out why this solution is so much more effective in their situation, to explain why it is so much better for them. And to get the person to see the solution overcomes and outweighs the pain that they feel in the change they have to make.

Another question is, "Why would I want to buy in this area of town?" Interestingly enough, you see this with people who are relocating. They know where they're going to work, and they draw a circle. They look at everything and anything within that circle. And here's the secret, when they move to the new city, they would like some things to be the same as they had before. Even if they go into this new place and gain new experiences, they still want some things that felt like home. Do you know what home feels like? Do you know why they live in the area that they currently live in? Do you know why they like it? Why are they considering these different areas? Those are all essential facts to know. So, you have the ability then to present how you match up.

People also want to know why, "I wouldn't want to buy in this particular neighborhood." Now, those of you in the new home business are wondering why didn't she say community? That's what we call it. I look at this a little differently. I don't want to live in a commune. I want to live in a place where I have neighbors. That's what we're looking for, a neighborhood. What does my life look like on the weekends? And at night, after I come home from a long day of work and I shut that front door, what does life look like? Living in this particular neighborhood, some people are looking for safety, some people are looking for friends for their children, some people say I don't need friends, I just want to be left alone. It's different for every person.

Another question they want answered would be, "Why would I want to buy a home on this particular lot? What's the orientation of the home? What's around it?" This is so much easier for those of us who have any kind of a home that's already existing. Whether it's a resale or an inventory home, if it's already there, it's a whole lot easier to see. But if I have to build a home for someone, what's the vision, "What will my backyard look like? Where will my neighbors be? Where will the sunset be at night? Do I want to pool?" All of those things will become increasingly important as you go along.

And then the last question they need to answer is, "Why would I even want to buy today? Why would I want to act on this instead of waiting or looking further?"

We're going to create a demonstration that helps your prospects get some of these answers to their questions by bringing some of these topics up, but let's start at the very beginning. Let's talk about the brain. The brain has so much to do with how we think. We have two parts of our brain, the conscious and the subconscious. The conscious part of our brain can only filter so many bits of information at a time, while the subconscious brain can exponentially filter so many more bits of information. So, what does your brain do? Your brain hacks itself!

The subconscious looks for anything that looks similar or repetitive, and the minute it sees repetition, it says, great. I know how this goes. "Conscious mind, go ahead and work on something else. I've got this problem handled." Don't believe me. Let me use this example. One day, you're driving home from work just like you do every single day, just having a conversation on the phone with your friend. You pull in the driveway, and you realize at that moment you actually have no idea of how you got there. Think about it this way. If you're driving along and suddenly there's an accident ahead, your subconscious sees red lights flashing and all of a sudden like, boom, you put your foot on the brakes, why? Because your subconscious said, "Hey, conscious mind, something's going on up here. I don't know how this works. You better get involved on the trip that you've taken eight zillion times home from the office."

Your subconscious knows where it goes, how it goes, where to turn. It had taken over your thoughts, given that you made the trip almost every day, and the result is you end up in your driveway. So, the very first thing you need to understand is that what you say to a customer when you first meet them is critically important. If what you say sounds like something any other realtor or any other salesperson you've known has said, you just created an opportunity for the conscious mind to sit back and the subconscious mind to take over because that's what it does. The buyer doesn't intend to stop listening to you. It's just what our brains do. So, if you want to keep them consciously involved and really involved in the conversation with you, you've got to stop saying what other people say.

If I see a realtor demonstrating a house, a lot of times, they'll walk in and say, "Here's the dining room, here's the living room," like I couldn't figure that out myself. Same thing with those of you in new home sales, "What brought you in today? Did you happen to see one of our signs?" We all ask these questions. And some of you are probably feeling ashamed. Maybe you're laughing. We've all done these things. And as a result, we have absolutely put a person in a trance. They're not paying attention to us. They're just giving us answers. So how about having a conversation that looks very different? The very first thing I would suggest that you do is start talking to that prospect about what they know. Think about it. If I start talking to you about what you know, I'm already giving you the recognition that I think you're an intelligent savvy research buyer. Wow. Guess what you're doing? You're actually making me feel good about myself. You're complimenting me without complimenting me. Oh, that's a piece of likability. I like people who compliment me.

Here's an example of how that questioning might go considering that most people I've talked to have done some research already, either online or they've driven around, gone to open houses, whatever the case may be. So, I might ask, "Would you mind sharing with me what research you've already done?" Now they go ahead and tell me what they know and then I'm going to repeat that back to them. If you repeat back to someone their same words it shows that you are actively listening to them. I get the question all the time, "Won't they think I'm making fun of them?" No, they don't even realize what you're doing. Some of the things related to likeability have to do with people thinking you sound like them. They like you because you must be like them. So, I'm going to repeat back what they told me and confirm, "Is that right? Have I got that? Yes, absolutely." Okay. And then my second question is, "How can I make the time you spend with me the most valuable? What one or two things were you hoping to learn today that would make this visit helpful for you?" For those of you who really want to be of service, I applaud you for having the servant's heart. You can't be a better servant to somebody than to ask them what they want to accomplish, not give them what you think they need to know. That's the problem with most salespeople, telling people what they think they need to know. By instead showing the person that I am actively listening to them, I made that person feel important because I've given them props for what they already know. It also helps me because I know how educated they are and now I know what I'm working with. It helps me qualify where I need to go in my sales presentation. All of those things are hugely important.

Now let's bridge the gap because here's where most people fall down. "How do I demonstrate this particular home to someone?" Hmm. Why is that so hard? Well, because unfortunately, a lot of home builders have decided that in demonstrating a home, what I'm going to focus on is a couple of things. Number one I have a lot of upgrades in my model. So, I'm going to go ahead and tell you, I need to walk you through the house and show you what's standard and what's an upgrade. Ooh, bad idea. I know that flies in the face of what many have told me, but now all the customer is doing is adding and adding and adding. Before you're done walking through the house, they now think they can't afford it because everything's an upgrade. Let's face it. You have a model home. How many times has anybody taken every upgrade you have in that model home? Very rarely. A lot of them don't even like some of the things they've done in the model.

For example, what's popular today is a lot of those upper cabinets with glass doors. I have a really, really good friend who is an excellent decorator. And she changes out everything behind those glass doors for every holiday. Every time I go over to her house, it's fabulous. Not my house. I don't need anybody to see the plastic cups I've been saving for 20 years. I don't need everybody to see the dust on my grandmother's cut glass crystal that I haven't dusted up there. So, a feature upgrade that is obviously important to my friend is not necessarily important to me. My first question is, would that be something that's important to this current buyer? I'll make a note of it. I don't even talk about pricing at that point. If those glass door cabinets are not an upgrade, then I can say, "Well, that's great because here's what our standard is." And now they're happy. So, don't focus on the upgrade opportunity.

What if you meet someone and tell them you are just going to walk through the model with them in case they have any questions. "You're creeping me out," is what the buyer's thinking. "You just want to follow me around to try to sell me something." It is the ultimate mistake. If you answer some initial questions and then just let them go, and then I meet up with them later, and here's what happens at the meetup. The prospective buyer goes through a couple of parts of the home. Usually, we meet back up in the family room after they've come out of the master. And the very first question is, "What do you think?"

"Well, the house is too big for me."

"Oh, not a problem. I have other homes that are smaller."

"That's okay. Thanks so much.

Or "The house is too small for me."

"I have other homes that are bigger."

"That's okay. No time today."

Here's the problem. Most people are walking through the home and then just ruling it out. Don't allow that to become a consideration step. If you are just letting them walk away, you have no idea what they're thinking.

I'll give you another example. We were shopping salespeople for a builder, and the builder sales rep had talked to the shoppers for a little bit and let them go look around the house while they got some materials together, and as I'm watching the video, the shoppers say to one another:

"Should we go back downstairs? Do you think she's going to come back up here?" Now think about this. This is a shopper who is supposed to talk to this person who is worried about when the salesperson is going to come back. If a shopper's doing that, don't you think prospective buyers are doing the same thing, but in a bad way? Why would you want anyone to ask, "Do you think she's going to come back?" So, this whole idea that if I let you go, that'll be a pressure reduction and you'll take more time is absolutely incorrect.

They're actually looking at how quickly they can leave the house because they're fearful of having to meet up with you anyway. This scenario has never worked. I want to be with that prospect all the way through their tour of the home, but how do I do that?

What I would say to somebody is if I'm a new home builder? First, most plans that you sell as a new home sales agent have options, meaning structural options. I would ask you, how many structural options does that plan have? Then multiply how many plans you have by how many average structural options you have. Let's say you have ten plans, and they have five structural options. Basically, I have 50 different ways to build a plan. It's not exact math, but it works for what I'm talking about. Prospective buyers like to have options but not be overwhelmed by them. I might say, "I have 50 different ways to build a house, and you don't want to go through all 50 different options. Let's walk through this one model, and let's look at it and see what you really like. And see if there are things about it that you don't like. Let's have a conversation about how you want to use these different areas. And when we're all done, I'm going to take all these different ways I could build a house, and I'm going to narrow all of these choices down to two or three options that make the most amount of sense for you to start with. Fair enough?" I ended with, fair enough.

If I say, fair enough, what am I doing? I'm creating a yes momentum because I laid out a very logical process for what we will do, and that requires the prospective customer to agree. I started the process by telling the customer what "most people have told me has been most successful or helpful for them." Everyone wants to replicate someone else's success. When I tell somebody that other people I work with found this approach we're going to use it to be the most helpful, they are more likely to stay with me.

The third important piece of information I told him is we've got 50 different options. I'm working on overwhelming them. Some of you have hundreds of different ways to build a house. I am saying, "We've got an overwhelming number of options for you. "I'm going to help you drill that down based on the conversation that we have." What am I doing? I'm setting the customer up to understand we will walk the entire home together for their benefit.

"I want you to understand how you're going to use these areas of the home. I want you to understand what you like. If there's something about a room that doesn't work, you can tell me that too. And then, with all the knowledge I have, I'm going to take all this information and drill it down to some options for you to start with. Does that sound fair to you?" If we work in this way, they have to answer yes. Everybody wants to be treated fairly and what I've just laid out is fair enough.

Now, as a realtor, I can do the same thing in an open house. I can do the same thing in showing any property. You have hundreds of listings that are available for you to show. So, as you're showing a house or your open house, you'd say, "I'd love to walk through this house and get a better understanding of what you like, what you're looking for. How this compares to what you have now because this listing may or may not work for you, but there are hundreds of other listings I could show you. And if I have a better idea, I can minimize your time spent and show you a couple of options that might work for you. Fair enough?" Again, I've earned the right to stay with this prospective buyer rather than having them turn around and look at me, thinking I am creeping them out because I'm following me from room to room.

What this also does, when they're telling me, "Well, I really don't like this about this room, I really wanted it more open," is to allow me to gain more valuable information. My first question is, "Compared to what?" They're obviously comparing this to something else now. What do I learn? "Well, I saw a house over at such and such a builder that had that" without ever asking them about the competition, I now know who I'm competing against. Maybe they say, "I saw a resale with this," or for my realtor friends, they may have seen a new home. That's your competition. Now you understand what ballpark you're playing in. You know what they've seen. You know what they like, and now they're able to show it to you. The other thing this does is allow people to stay engaged. All of you know the buyer is supposed to talk more than you, the salesperson. And yet, in all the years, I've done this. I have watched salespeople dominate 80% of the conversation and the customer about 20%. One of the things I always talk about with people I coach is, "Do you know more about the prospect at the end of the presentation? Or do they know more about you and your product?" It should be that you know more about them and what they're looking for, then potentially they know more about you because if they know more about you and your product, you've been talking way too much.

Part of the problem we have in presentations is we ask very closed-ended questions. Who, what, when, where, why, and how, right? Someone told you in training, those were open-ended questions. Now I happen to have taken journalism classes in college. Who, what, when, where, why, and how to apply to the five things you need to have in the first paragraph of the story that you write for a newspaper or a magazine. So, someone will know if they want to read the article. It has nothing to do with interviewing. And if you look at really great interviewers like Barbara Walters, for those of you who know who that is, if you don't go on YouTube and look up some of her interviews. She was a fabulous interviewer because she asked questions that started like, tell me, tell me more, help me understand. She didn't say, "How did you do this? What did you do?" Because asking who, what, when, where, why, and how, too easily gets a one-word answer. And if you get enough one-word answers at the end of the day, guess what? You stop asking questions and start tell-selling because people feel like they are being grilled by you; they don't like it. They're getting uncomfortable. You're not asking great questions.

So, what this process does is it allows us to get the buyer to feel like they are leading when in fact, we're controlling the entire conversation. Think about it. If you're showing a kitchen, how cool is it for them to open a cabinet and talk about adjustable shelves? How cool is it to have somebody stand behind the kitchen sink, and then you begin to understand that they have big family parties and they do a lot of cooking? You start staging people in the kitchen to see if the kitchen is big enough to accommodate everybody. People want to play. People want to be involved. And nine times out of ten, what they're stuck doing is standing there while we talk at them. How boring is that? Or they're just wandering through a house, trying to figure it out.

For my builder friends, here's one of the big mistakes I often see. The buyer says to you, "Can we move that window?" For those of you who can make personal changes for people, what do you answer? "Oh, sure. We can do that." The buyer's really saying to you something about that window location doesn't work. The response needs to be, "I'm sensing there's something about that window location that doesn't work for how you want to decorate. What kind of wall space are you needing?" Remember, new home salespeople, we're not trying to sell our model. We're trying to get a feel for what people need so that we can put them in the right floor plan. It's easy for a person to walk through a model. And what they're doing when they're asking if they can make changes is they're telling you the model doesn't work for them. Because they think your model is pretty and they can visualize the space, they're trying to figure out how they can change it to make it work for them. I guarantee you, you have a plan that works way better for them. The model is not always the best option. Same thing holds true for my realtor friends. When people start saying, "Oh, this is pretty dark in here." You should be asking, "Tell me some of the reasons you feel like it's so dark compared to what you were hoping for?" Or, "Tell me some of the things you were hoping for, so I get a better feel for it." Maybe there's a simple alteration that can be made, like changing the paint color. Maybe it tells me they really need to be looking at a different house. It really helps us to determine what the buyer's needs are.

Here's the basic premise that causes us to make assumptions and fail in our help for buyers. We assume that every buyer sits down at their kitchen table with their spouse or their significant other, or even just by themselves, and starts having a conversation about what's important in a house. "Where do we want the TV location? When we're standing at the sink, do we want it directly across the room? Or do we want it at an angle? What do you really want to have happen in this bedroom?" You know, "Do I need to have a place for the TV here? Or do I not want the TV in the bedroom? Where are you going to hang your clothes in the closet? Are you sure that you have enough room for the clothes? And do you want double racks?" These are not conversations people have or questions they have considered before they show up. There's something about the house that doesn't work. It's not big enough. It's too small, Blah, blah, blah. Before you know it, that's what we're going off to the races with. And here's the challenge when they come in and we ask questions, like how many bedrooms were you hoping for? Four bedrooms? One story or two story, two story? What's your price range? 350 to 400. Guess what? Every other salesperson has asked these questions, but even worse, the fact that they have come in telling you these are the things they must have in a home before you even ask any questions, and they're still in the market looking says the solution they're telling you doesn't solve their problem. Let me repeat that to you. The solution they're telling you they're looking for doesn't solve the problem. Let me illustrate this point.

There was a salesperson that I worked with at one point in time. His sales manager was telling me this story, and we'll call him John. John said, "Oh, I have these buyers who are absolutely going to want to buy a house. They really want to downsize. They really wanted a smaller yard. And they just had to think through a couple of things. They're supposed to be back tomorrow."

The sales manager said, "What'd you say their name was?"

John told her what the name was. And she said, "Well, I'm sorry, John, they won't be back tomorrow."

He said, "why is that?"

She said, "Because they already bought a house in one of our other neighborhoods."

They didn't buy a smaller house. They bought a bigger house. They didn't buy a house on a smaller lot. They bought a house on a big cul-de-sac lot. And guess what? They spent a hundred thousand dollars more for the house then they said they were going to spend for any of the homes you showed them.

You all know what I'm talking about. You have people that come in and tell you what they want. And then you follow up with them because you haven't heard from them in a while and you find out they bought something totally different than what they told you they had to have. It proves my point. Why would you only want to ask questions like bedroom count, bathroom count, one story, two story, square footage. It's not enough. If that's the only information you're getting, 9 times out of 10, you're going to have the wrong solution for their problem.

You have to start your presentation in a way that no one else is starting it. Start your presentation by complimenting the buyer, talking about the research they've done. This will actually help you understand how savvy of a buyer they are. It will tell you an enormous amount of the kind of presentation you're going to have to do. Imagine if they said to you, "This is the first place we've looked at," what do you think you have to do compared to somebody who says, "We've looked at 15 houses," very, very different education level. Very different about what they know about the market. We can then explain to people that we're going to take them through a process that others have found unsuccessful for them.

We walk them through the house and look at cabinets. We look at cabinet sizes. We look at the length of countertops. We look at layouts. We look at where TVs go. We look at where functions can happen. We look at traffic flow, we look at all these things, and then we take all the options that we have and start narrowing it down for people. And then, at the end of this, we're going to then present the options based on all of the things we've taken notes on. That's an important piece. You got to take notes. You can't keep this in your brain. There's no way you're going to keep this in your brain.

The other piece of this is when we have all these notes written down, we're going to sit down with these people and go over all the things they told us. They don't remember what they told you, so we have a process of showing them the options that we think are best for them. Do you see how different this presentation style is? This is very different than telling them everything your builder does that no one else does. There's an opportunity walking from room to room to ask questions like, "What's going to be most important to you and your family. Tell me more about the kind of neighborhood you want to put your family in." Wow. How much could I learn? There are many different ways you can have a conversation, and truly a great demonstration is about a great conversation, not a presentation.

ACTION STEPS:

- First, I would suggest all of you record your presentation as it is today. Before you try to make any changes, put your phone on record in your pocket and listen to what you say. I know it's appalling. Stop spending time with the distractions.

LISTEN to the content and not the delivery! That being said, if I understand my presentation, then step two is I can start to refine my presentation.

- I'm not asking you to throw the baby out with the bathwater. If your questions aren't good, then figure out what your question's intention is and rewrite it. You get better answers when you take that step to rewrite questions, listen to your presentation, rewrite your presentation.

- Grade yourself on where you think you are and be really brutally honest. The more brutally honest you are with yourself and where you have opportunities to improve, the quicker you can take action on the improvements you need to make.

- Practice, practice, practice. This is where most people fail. They think this type of demonstration is a great idea. When I show it to them, they love it. I present it to them, and they take notes on it and then never try to make it theirs. Here's the problem. If you don't practice it, it won't become second nature. If it doesn't become second nature, you're going to trip all over yourself. And as a result, it won't be effective. And when it's not effective, you're going to say to me, this process doesn't work.

CHAPTER FOUR

The Generational Conversations

AS WE DISCUSSED IN THE previous chapter, the dollars are in the demonstration. How well you do at getting a buyer to understand their needs, not just wants and desires, and to be able to define those needs and wants and desires is crucial to define the right solutions for their problems. That being said, there are also things we are talking about as well during that conversation, like the reputation of our company or the reputation of the business that we've created. We will be talking about how we converse about this in the future. There's a lot of other things we're going to rely upon during that conversation that is very dependent on the generation the buyer belongs to.

As you'll find out in this chapter, different generations are not created equal. Nor are they the same in how they communicate or how they view information. They certainly won't have the same thoughts about how they view the conversation they have with you.

Here is a perfect example. My husband is a baby boomer, late-stage baby boomer, and he hates technology. In fact, whenever he touches a piece of technology, like a phone, a computer, whatever it may be, it always ends up zoning out on him or having a problem. I don't have the same problems with my technology that he does. Of course, he hates technology. So, my husband, who is in his late sixties, has told me and everyone around him in no uncertain terms, he refuses to text. Now I should go back and say, this was also the man that when I met him, said he would never have a computer in the house back in the late 1990s. Well, that certainly changed. We have a computer, in fact more than one. He's been very proud of himself for the fact that he refuses to text, and anyone that knows him knows that's the case. My stepson married a couple of years ago, and he is married to a millennial woman, I would say late-stage millennial, maybe early Gen Xer. But anyway, she has totally given up calling on the phone. That's not her method of any kind of conversation. So interestingly enough, for my husband's birthday, a couple of years ago, I got a text from my daughter-in-law, who said to me she just wanted to wish dad a happy birthday. And since she doesn't call and he won't text, she texted me to tell him happy birthday from her!

I think that's the best indication of how different generations look at communication and what's important to them, and how they converse. So, let's start talking about these different generations and how we can converse with them. The very first ones I want to talk about are called the traditionalists. They were born before 1946. These people were shaped by some very extreme events. For example, they lived through World War II. My mom happens to be a traditionalist. She was the youngest of four children and a late in life child for my grandparents. She saw very little of her oldest brother when she was young because he was in the military, and so was her second brother.

This demographic was the first group to really start coming in from rural America, coming into bigger cities to get employment because you started to have manufacturing due to World War II. You had a lot of different things begin to happen in the cities, and people made that transition from rural farm areas to cities. Wow, what a difference! They also faced prohibition. I hope most of you know what that is, but in case you don't, it was during this time that the United States government decided that there should be no alcohol sold. So, these people learn to live without that option in life. They also lived through the Great Depression, not the great recession of the early 2000s, but the Great Depression. My mother was a typical product of the Great Depression. My grandfather lost his job. They lost their house. They were forced to have to find a rental property. My dad, on the other hand, his father worked in a meatpacking plant. And so, he kept his job through the Great Depression. They had food on the table. They got to bring things home from the meatpacking plant. My mom was very fortunate in that my grandfather found work to keep him busy. And so, they continued to be fed, but they lost their home. And also, during this time, they saw the creation of the atomic bomb. If you remember your history lessons, the atom bomb was dropped on two cities in Japan in order to end the Pacific conflict part of World War II.

Think about all of those different things that happened to them. Ask them what kind of TV shows they watched. They didn't. There was no TV; trick question. They listened to the radio, and everyone gathered around the radio. They listened to a lot of half-hour programs. A company always sponsored these half-hour programs. And if you listen to some of those old radio shows, that sponsor was able to give about a five-minute talk about their product, how the product could be used, and how it would benefit someone in their life. As a result, these traditionalists saw advertising as actual education about a product, not as a sales pitch.

The baby boomer, on the other hand, was born sometime between 1946 and 1964. Now, in this generation, one of the key events that shaped their view of the world was they saw the biggest and most robust economic expansion ever in the history of America; there were jobs to go around. What happened is after World War II was over, much of Europe was devastated. All the manufacturing plants in America still kept rolling. No longer were they making war time materials, but now they manufactured other things. Manufacturing took off in the biggest way in the United States. They also saw the advent of television. They were the first generation to see anything on TV. I am a boomer, and I can still remember the very first color TV I ever saw; I was in high school. In those days, there were only three channels, and they all went off at midnight every night. There was no such thing as TV 24 hours a day, seven days a week. We saw the civil rights movement in the mid-sixties. We got to watch Martin Luther King. We were able to watch so many different figures talk about the different civil rights opportunities. Many of the divisions between people were suddenly now working towards being mended. My generation also faced the Vietnam war. I grew up in a high school where a lot of my friends in high school were actually drafted and served over there. I was in the ninth grade and one of my best friend's brothers was in the Vietnam war. So, from fourth grade all the way until I was a freshman in college, I experienced the Vietnam war in one way or another.

We saw Watergate in 1972. If you remember that from history, you know President Nixon sent people into the Democratic National Party offices to steal information. That was one of the first big political uproars. And we also saw the United States and the USSR limit nuclear warhead testing. When I was in grade school, we were taught to hide underneath our desks in case of a nuclear attack. There were bomb shelters for nuclear attacks. You were taught what to do and where to go.

We watched very value-oriented TV shows like *Gunsmoke, Bonanza, Andy Griffith, Marcus Welby, MD*, things like that. So, our generation was very, very different from what we saw from the traditionalists. Most baby boomers see themselves as having a very strong work ethic. They see themselves as very competent in their careers. Their career defines them, and they define their career. They believe they're ethical, take responsibility for their actions and believe they're communicators. Interestingly enough, the baby boomer generation saw the surge in the divorce rate because so many women could now have jobs. Since baby boomer women could get good-paying jobs, they no longer needed to stay in a marriage that didn't work.

We also started to think that old age began at about 80 years old, rather than the traditionalist who saw old age creeping in at 65. They're very affluent. Baby boomers believed they were very special in their abilities and in their opportunities. Interestingly enough, in 2011, the median retirement savings for a baby boomer was only $40,000 because what did baby boomers do? They grew up with very little of nothing. As a result, they became the me generation and spent it all on themselves.

TV allowed us to see the world together. As I mentioned, there were only three stations. Everything that was on the news was projected at the same time. We all saw Kennedy's death. We all saw John F. Kennedy's funeral. We all saw the same things at the same time.

Baby boomers were the generation that first started moving away from hanging out with their folks. The very first thing I wanted to do at 18 was get a job and move out of the house. They're very skeptical of the government. They became very skeptical of politicians. They were willing to sacrifice for their own self-fulfillment. You saw generations now willing to work at the expense of their family. So consequently, you saw many, many children of the baby boomer population spend a lot of time at home by themselves because mom and dad were both working. They're idealistic versus pragmatic, and they value communication.

Let's move on to Gen X. Gen Xers were born between 1965 and 1980. What events shaped their thought process? Double-digit inflation. For the first time, we saw inflation rates of over 12 and 13%. We started to see the very first technology that was in people's hands. The Sony Walkman and MTV both came on the scene. Think about that, for those of you who remember that, watching music all the time on one channel. You started to see a new set of channels as cable TV started to take over, and you started to see more opportunities for entertainment. 1989 saw the Berlin wall come down. So, the idea of a communist party or a communist type of society was not a concern. They didn't experience that like the baby boomer generation that believed the Russians were going to drop a bomb on us any given day. And they also experienced in the early 2000s the Gulf War almost as if it were a TV show. TV became more realistic and a lot less value oriented. For example, *Dallas, The Simpsons* that first cartoon type of entertainment, while other shows were poking fun at everyday life like *Friends* and *Seinfeld.* Think about the aspects of those shows and how different that would look from the *Andy Griffith Show* or *Bonanza.*

The Gen Xers also see themselves as very confident, competent, and ethical. They also take responsibility for their actions. But the difference here is they don't put in extra time to complete a project, whereas the baby boomer does. This population is 25% smaller than boomers. They were stuck behind the baby boomer generation. In fact, baby boomers have created a problem called the white ceiling. Because so many baby boomers don't want to retire at 65, they're staying in the same jobs longer. Gen Xers are now left without a road to move up. Baby boomers had two kids, one, or none. As I said, the divorce was commonplace with baby boomers and as a result about 29% of these Gen Xers did not grow up with both parents.

They learned to adjust because a lot of their time at home was spent alone because both parents worked, or they were a product of a one parent household. Their friends became their support system. This is where the term latchkey child comes from. These Gen X kids would come home from school and let themselves into their locked home. They were left to their own devices to do their homework, perhaps to make dinner for their family, to clean the house, or to help care for their brothers and sisters. They had a lot of responsibility placed upon them. The focus became family versus work. 40% of the class of 1990 in this group had no job when they left college.

The last generation we need to talk about is the millennials. They've always wanted success, but nothing has ever come easy for them. They grew up with technology. Computers were commonplace as they were growing up. They understand technology in a way that no one else does. They grew up as the computer age generation. With so much additional information, they began to question and verify everything. Our millennial generation was born between the years of 1981 and 2001. This generation has been molded by some very disturbing social events. They have watched the Oklahoma City bombing. They've seen the Columbine High School shooting. They've lived through 9-11. They also have experienced the Great Recession and the slowest job recovery that our economy has ever seen. The millennial generation has been shaped by a lot of hardship, not to mention the fact that the society for our millennials has changed.

For baby boomers, it was very safe. You could go anywhere. In fact, I'll tell a story about my husband. When he grew up, his mom had three children, all within basically three years of each other. So, when it was the weekend, and they were old enough, they'd say, "Hey mom, we're going to go camping."

She said, "Great. See you by Sunday dinner."

And they were gone. Nobody worried about where kids were during that time. That has changed drastically today. You would certainly not tell some child, go ahead, go to the playground, go ahead and play, come home by dinner next Tuesday. You'd be afraid of what child molester may have picked them up along the way. As a result, millennials grew up with what we call helicopter parents. These parents, who are either baby boomers or Gen Xers, are ultra-concerned about kid safety and as a result, have stayed very close to them.

As I said before, their parents have a huge role to play in their life because they just couldn't go to the playground and play. Parents found ways to be active with their children. What started to happen? Select baseball, select soccer, cheerleading. In baby boomer days, you were only a cheerleader, or on the football team or the baseball team or a volleyball team or the soccer team if the school had a team and you tried out and made it.

Parents want these children to have an opportunity to be with others, so they go to organized sporting events. The parents spend a lot of time with their children. They have a lot of drive time; they had a lot of windshield time to talk about a lot of things. Interestingly enough, 50% of the millennials that were interviewed said they see their parents as role models. Wow. That's way different than the baby boomers who wanted to get out of the house at 18. Millennials also tend to say their parents are some of their best friends. Dialogue was extremely important. They've been told all along that they can do something great. For the 20 years of their life growing up, they have been their parents' center of attention. As a result, they're actually some of the savvier consumers because they've been raised as consumers. They've been taught what to ask for, and if you can't get it, look someplace else. More than 50% of them also drop out of college before earning a degree. That's an interesting topic because the cost to go to college has been very expensive. And a lot of them said, "I don't need this degree to help me get to where I need to go." For our millennials, happiness rates higher than money.

You might be thinking that this is all really interesting, but how does this really affect sales? Let's talk about it. I have 12 different points we'll discuss. The first is communication. And when I say that, what's the vehicle for communication and what are their rules for etiquette? The traditionalist prefers mail, snail mail. Yeah. You heard it. They like getting letters in the mailbox. They prefer things by mail. They're more technologically savvy than they used to be, so they do now rely on email. If you see them on Facebook, it's really only to check out their grandkids. It's not a place for them to grab information. And they're hesitant to learn about a lot of things on the internet. They also believe that people will say things online that they wouldn't say in person. So that's why some of these online platforms aren't the best when talking to a Traditionalist.

The baby boomer prefers the phone. They are very data-centric. If you're going to try to sell them a home or work with them on buying a home, they want to have a conversation. In fact, they really prefer personal conversations, especially when they're spending a lot of money, but the phone will be okay. They really don't want you to email them. They will take a text from time to time. Still, most baby boomers do not believe that texting is the way to communicate business information.

Gen Xers prefer emails that are very concise with bullet points. They like to scan. And because our Gen Xers are a little bit skeptical about the world, they also like to have everything in writing because if something goes wrong, they want to be able to pull that back up and share that with you, good or bad.

The millennial, on the other hand, prefers texting. They're really not phone callers. And most millennials you talk with may have an email account, but they rarely look at it.

When making a decision, traditionalists defer to experts. Remember I said they listened to radio programs. The person who was doing the five-minute advertisement was seen as an expert on the product they were selling. Good news for you as a salesperson, they deem you as having valuable information because you are an expert.

The baby boomer likes you have to have done some exhaustive research to show them why this is a good decision for them. They will also look at you as a salesperson as a professional. The baby boomer sees sales as a profession, so they do respect what you have to say.

A Gen Xer is going to look at whoever is the most qualified to decide. That's why they do a lot of research on the internet. They look for a lot of help from decision-makers on information from the internet. A Gen Xer will go to a specific site. They will look for great resources, but they won't necessarily put that out to everybody asking for their opinion.

Millennials like to be broad and inclusive, and if their preferences are ignored, they leave you. For example, a millennial will put something out on the internet on Facebook about needing a babysitter for Thursday night. "Anybody got any recommendations?" Well, I will tell you, as a baby boomer, there's no way any of us would have put that out on social media because we would think everybody knew we were gone, and our kids were alone with someone they didn't know. We would say, "Who vetted these people?"

Third part of communication is feedback. For our traditionalist, no news equals good news. Think about it. They grew up during World War II. If somebody came to your door to talk to you about something or made a phone call, it wasn't to communicate good news. It wasn't to have a chit chat. It was to tell you something bad. So, when you're trying to give them any kind of information or they're giving you feedback, no news is pretty much good news on their behalf.

Boomers like feedback to be very formal. They like it to be succinct. They like it to be factual. And they like it to be data-driven.

Gen Xers like feedback to be real-time and uncomplicated, giving the facts, just the facts. They want you to just tell it to them.

Millennials, on the other hand, prefer a coaching mentality. Remember, if they've spent a lot of time with their parents and their parents have treated them as basically a contemporary, they've always had conversations as if they were equals. So, if you had the salesperson try to take an approach of talking down to you because you've never bought a home before, or the salesperson believes you don't know what you're doing, the salesperson is going to lose you in a heartbeat. Millennials want you to coach them and talk to them as equal.

All generations want fun, especially the millennials. This is how you resolve to make it fun. The traditionalist relaxes when all the work is done. So, when you're giving a presentation, don't be funny. Don't be humorous. Let's get the work done. And when we're all done, we can sit back and say, "Okay, we got it all finished."

The baby boomer believes that work is fun. So, as they're working through this process with you buying, it is fun for them. The facts you provide are fun. The homework they need to do is all fun.

The Gen Xer wants to quit trying to make it something it's not. So, if you're trying to make this sale look like it's not a sales presentation, they do not believe you. So, don't even try. They understand this is a presentation. They see that at some level, there's a value to it. So, let's be real. The millennial believes everything should be fun. So, when you're working with them, if you're talking fact, fact, fact, or driving too much data, or you're doing too much education, it will no longer be fun. It will be work, and you will lose their attention.

How do we transfer knowledge? The traditionalist likes to watch your presentation and listen to you and the baby boomers much the same. Remember, they respect a sales professional as a professional in their jobs. So, they will allow you to give a presentation and value what you let them know.

The Gen Xer prefers a frequently asked question or FAQ type of presentation. They prefer it to be oral or written. So just the facts, put it out there FAQ style. And before you know it, you'll have them right where you need them.

Millennials like to have knowledge transferred to them in a fun way. These people love videos. They don't have to be picture-perfect videos. In fact, quite frankly, if you do a video that's too perfect, a millennial or Gen Xer might question whether or not you're really lying to them. They like things to be organic. They like it to look spur of the moment. Remember, this is the fun group. If you want to get them information, make sure you get the information to them in a fun way.

How about loyalty? How loyal are these buyers? Traditionalists and baby boomers are very loyal. The boomer is very loyal to the cost and the benefits of changing. So he is going to be looking at any home sale or purchase as, "Is the cost of what I'm having to go through worth the benefit of what I'm going to get?"

The Gen Xer says, "Will I come out the other end surviving this?"

Millennials say, "I want to like the people. I want it to be pleasant. And I want to feel like I'm satisfied with the presentation."

How about meetings? If you're going through buying a home or building a home for someone or selling a home for someone, and there's an issue that comes up, traditionalists and baby boomers want a meeting face to face. If there's a problem and they're spending as much money as they are for a home, they want to see you in person. They want you to have a conversation with them in person.

The Gen Xer will do a face-to-face, but they want that to be supplemental to the email. Remember to give them the facts. They want all of it spelled out in bullet points because they want to keep this in their bible of everything that you told them. They may need to use it against you at some point in time because remember, they are skeptical.

Millennials love face to face. So how do you do face to face since they like technology? Facetime or Zoom Meeting platforms are fabulous for the millennial. They love to have those kinds of meetings. They love meetings to be interactive.

What about policies? All of us have policies and procedures in what we do. The traditionalist will always obey the rule. Remember, you're the expert. If this is how it goes, this is what I'll do. The baby boomer will follow policies and rules because they understand it's what makes business run fairly and smoothly.

Now the Gen Xer on the other hand says rules are made to be broken. I had a scenario once where I was working with a construction manager who had a Gen X client and the Gen Xer wanted to make some modifications to the house. Well, they were at a stage of construction where modification really shouldn't have been made. At the very beginning, I should add this, the Gen Xer was very, very demanding about a finish date because they had a special needs child, and they didn't want to have their special needs child in a position where they had to be moved multiple times. Totally understand that. They wanted to make a change by adding insulation to a media room. Here's an interesting aside. They had gone to their local Best Buy and talked to a salesperson who might've been 22 or 23, and this salesperson told them how they should best soundproof a media room. The Best Buy salesperson had never built a home before. This was just their approach. So, when this Gen Xer came to the builder, they didn't ask the builder, "Should we go ahead and insulate this media room the best way," they just told them what the salesperson said to him. That was fine because that was their new expert. Well, we have a baby boomer builder who says, "That's not our policy."

What did I just say? Gen Xers believe policies are made to be broken. But that was not going to work for the baby boomer builder. His policy did not allow changes. So, he told the Gen Xer, "Why would you think that the guy selling media equipment at Best Buy is the best person to tell you how to do the installation of this media room, especially if you need this house done quicker?" You can see where this builder went wrong in so many different ways. What the builder should have said is, "Wow, that's very interesting. I hadn't heard that before about insulating a media room. Could I call your salesperson and talk to him about his perceptions of this? Why he would recommend this based on the equipment you're going to get. And then both of us together can come up with the best solution for you." I would have also said to the Gen Xer, "Help me understand, which is the biggest priority. If we make these changes now we have a problem because I won't be able to meet the all-important conclusion date. So, are we willing to pass the completion date to get what you want, or is the completion date more important? Please let me know what works best for you." Imagine how much differently that solution would have looked and how much differently that Gen Xer would have looked at that builder had that conversation been done in this way.

The millennial says they just like guidelines. Now, if those guidelines don't make sense to them, they're not going to follow them.

How about respect? The traditionalist respects you for your position. So do baby boomers. Gen Xers will give you respect, if you prove you deserve it. And millennials will give you respect if you take them seriously. Millennials are first about themselves and then about you. They want a big picture, and they can't see that big picture until you help them see it. They want to know why before what. So, with that millennial, it's all about what you want to do, before why you want to do it. They want to be able to express themselves.

For Gen Xers information equals power. Give the Gen Xer the power. What do I mean by that? Go ahead and give them different websites they can refer to so they can gather the knowledge that they're going to need on their own. They're going to go all over the internet and you and I both know, just because it's on the internet, doesn't make it true. Pick two good sites, send them to get factual information; send them to a place that helps them. The more information they have, the better they like it, be willing to share, and explain the information.

The traditionalist makes decisions on how it affects them. How will their life be affected by what we're going to do today? baby boomers are all about what's in it for me. If they don't see that particular home as being a big benefit to them, they're on down the road. The Gen Xer says, "What do I need to do to survive this process?" While the millennial says, "What do I get out of this? And what do my friends get as well?" It's all about "me and the community."

So, as you can see, it's very important to understand these different generations and then put together a really great and dynamic communication and action plan based on their values and their communication styles. One of the biggest problems I see for most people when they're not getting along with a buyer is they decided to communicate in a way that's easiest for them, the salesperson, the realtor, rather than the way that it's best to communicate with the buyer. The more you make it about the buyer, the more you make it simple for them to work with you, the better chances you will have of getting them to make the right decision.

In this chapter, we talked a lot about the different conversations we have with different generations. Here are some action steps you can take to start adding those specific conversations to what you normally do with your customers.

ACTION PLAN:

- I understand it's very difficult to try to figure out sometimes what years people were born. But what I do know is that the better the conversation that you have, the easier it becomes. Obviously, you know, if I'm looking at a Traditionalist, they are going to be my older people. Millennials are a little bit easier, but there's a fine line between baby boomer and Gen Xer, or millennial and Gen Xer. However, based on all the information we outlined, see if you can't put in your presentation some great questions about their upbringing that will allow you to figure out what they are. For example, if I thought maybe they were a Gen Xer, I might talk about their first computer and where you used it in your home did you use it? If they say the very first thing I ever had was an Atari, then probably they're a Gen Xer because that was the very first type of computer out there.

So, suppose you ask some good questions about things they experienced in their life, growing up. In that case, it will help you pretty much identify what type of generational conversation you need to have to practice your conversations.

This may all make great sense when you read it, but if you don't practice how to put this into your presentation, it will be information that was helpful but never used.

- Set out an action plan for future communications with each one of these generations and how you will communicate with them. One thing I will add is about some traditionalists, they might actually use texts pretty well. I know my 86-year-old mother texts me quite frequently. Others like my husband, who is 68, won't touch a text. You can sort of find out some of the ways they like to communicate by asking a simple question. "What's the best way to communicate information to you?" That's very important. They'll usually tell you their preferred method of communication. You can also ask, "How long should I give you to respond before I try to reach you again?" That's also good because it puts them on notice that when you do send them something, you're going to be sending information that you're expecting a response to, not basic sales information.

- The last action step is make sure when you tell these people that you're going to communicate with them, tell them how you're going to communicate based on their communication style and what type of information you will be communicating with them on. Let them know it will be information related to questions you had.

It will be information that tells you more about our background. I will share with you other sources on the internet to get more information that will be helpful for you when you're making this decision. Again, the information that needs to be communicated needs to be directly related to how they make decisions. Still, they also now know that you're not going to fill their inbox or their voicemail or their text or whatever it may be with information that they do not want and do not want to read.

CHAPTER FIVE

Follow-up and Appointment Setting

INTERESTINGLY ENOUGH, follow-up is probably the most significant challenge salespeople have in today's world. When I work in coaching with my different sales clients, they are always confused when following up with people. In short, how to prioritize your prospects. What is a prospect, by the way? I will share three of them with you.

An A Prospect is willing, ready, and able to buy. A B Prospect only has two out of the three of the characteristics an A Prospect has. Maybe they're ready and willing, but not able, or they're able and willing, but not ready, or they're able and ready, but not willing. Lastly, a C Prospect is the person who has only one of those three: maybe they're ready, but not willing or able, maybe they're willing, but not ready or able, or maybe they're able, but not ready or willing.

Why do I put all that out there? Because what I've learned is that when we do a great demonstration, as we've discussed earlier, that is when we get the dollars. When we have a great demonstration, we get a lot of information about people. Interestingly enough, when I get information about prospects from my coaching clients, they can always identify A prospects. Why is that? Well, because they know a lot about them. It's the B and C prospects that we don't know so much about. Maybe we didn't hit it off. Maybe the conversation didn't go all that well. Maybe we had a phone call where we were trying to get an appointment. We thought things went okay but didn't get the warm and fuzzies.

I'll tell you about converting any prospect or following up with them… they should all be A prospects.

Every one of them probably is ready, willing, and able to buy at some level. Now, I know I'm going to get an argument from somebody that "they're not able if they can't afford the house." Well, maybe they're not able to afford the house that you're showing them at that price, but maybe they're able to afford something else.

Some people say they're not just ready, and I get that. They may come in and say, "We're going to buy a home in a year. We're just trying to get an idea of the marketplace." When people throw that out there, they're just putting you on pause. The rule of thumb is if they say they're a year out, they're really six months out. If they're six months out, the truth is it's really three months. And if they say three months out, they are really ready to buy today. Prospects don't want to let you know how soon they want to move because they don't want a salesperson pounding on them. They don't want that relentless follow-up. And as sales professionals we follow up all the time, don't we? I hear it all the time. "I just don't want to be a pest." "I just don't want to be considered a salesperson who is hounding people." I always say in response to that if you feel like you're a pest or hunting people, you don't have an excellent plan of action.

Many times, we already have the prospect in front of us. Maybe we're a realtor showing a property. Maybe we're a realtor with a listing presentation, having a conversation with somebody, or we're a new home salesperson. The prospect comes in, and we've gone through our demonstration. And then we realize that there is no sale going to be made today. Now I'm going to be a contrarian here. There are many people in this world today who still say that everyone can buy today. Well, is that true? Yeah, maybe. But the reality is people are a little more cautious now in their decision-making than years past. Years ago, you could close a deal with somebody in just one visit. Today, many of my business friends would tell you that if ever they were able to close a deal the same day the prospect first visited, 9 times out of 10, it's a bust. It busts out because people weren't really prepared to make a decision, or they said, "Wow, we should not have made a decision that quickly." And I would say to you that the higher the price tag on the sale, the more likely you are to have somebody at least want to go home overnight and have a conversation about it.

So what I really want you to do is think of it this way. I want to take every person through the sales process as far as they will let me go. Now, what does that mean? That means when I start to see them lose their interest, hopping from foot to foot with their arms crossed, I've probably given them as much information as they can possibly digest. Don't try to switch topics to get them reinvigorated. That's the time to stop. That's the time to strategize and set up the next appointment.

So many of my friends in this business are always on the phone or texting or emailing, trying to get people to come back out when actually the most straightforward thing they could have possibly done was set the appointment while someone was already there. What are some strategies for the next appointment? Well, the very first thing I can tell you is that you can give your buyer homework. I would send my prospect home and say, "Here's what I'd like you to do. I would like you to go home and really start taking a look at all the furniture you have in your current home or apartment or whatever it may be and decide what you're going to keep."

When people buy a new home, they also get new pieces of furniture. You gave your buyer homework; that is to decide what things are they going to keep when moving. With that, you can tell them to take some pictures of the things that will be kept and take measurements and send those back to you. For those of you who sell new homes, you can get access to actual plans that have the real dimensions, where you can actually start to sketch out the placement of furniture. And I would tell my buyers, "You know, everybody has different furniture. They have different sizes. They want it to accommodate different things. Let's make sure we know what we are working with. I'm going to do some research here as well. Let's make sure that what you want to keep fits in the rooms. Maybe there are some pieces of furniture that they're going to keep that would require them to have to look at a different plan to get a wall space that will accommodate it." I say to them, "Let's do that now." What does that do for somebody? It starts to really make them feel the pain of where they currently live. Because when you start getting them to look at furniture that they want to get rid of, what does that do? They say to themselves, "I can't stand this sofa anymore. I can't wait to get rid of it." It starts to create internal or intrinsic motivation to make a decision to move because the person starts to create more pain about their current situation.

So many people try to make the pain an external point of view. It's an internal motivator. It's something people have to experience themselves. Send them home, looking at what they don't like and what they want to change. On the flip side, I say to them, "Now what you should also do is whatever furniture you think you want to change, go ahead and start looking at what you would replace it with." And I would say, "Obviously, don't go buy that today, but what would you replace it with? Send me some of those pictures and get some measurements so we can make sure when we're looking at these different rooms that we can accommodate everything you're envisioning for this home." You think they're more interested in what you have? And this is the cool part, you sent them home continuing to think about moving and continuing to think about putting themselves in some of the homes you have.

Now, I know we've kind of come up with a plan. Maybe we did. Maybe we only got through the presentation to a point where we sent them home with a couple of plans to look at, but we didn't determine which is the right home for them. Then I would be saying, "You know, you've got those plans to look at, let me do some digging. Let me see if there's a plan that I missed. Let me see if there's something that we offer that I haven't thought of. Let me talk to my sales manager and see if based on everything you've told me see if she has an idea I haven't thought of. It'll take me a couple of days to get that done. Plus, I will go ahead and get my hands on the actual architectural plans for this home so we can sit down and sketch it out." (I'll tell you how to do that in a minute.) "If we sketch it out, then we can see if this plan works or if we need to make a change to a different plan."

Now, what about that appointment? People want to come back for appointments where they think they're going to have fun, where they feel like that they're going to get more information. They're not necessarily interested in coming back to an appointment that says they're going to get sold. And unfortunately, that's what we're trying to do when we set the appointment. We don't want to make them feel like that's the only agenda item we have, is to sell them something.

What do we actually have to do to help them move into a home? Well, you can go to a number of different websites and you would want to buy a furniture template. Yes, there are a lot of them and you'll either get one on an eighth inch scale or one on a quarter inch scale, depending on the architectural plans you use, do you use quarter inch scale plans or eighth inch scale plans? Buy yourself some tracing paper. When they come in, you rip off a piece of tracing paper. You place it over the plan and suddenly you can draw furniture in. We can get a feel for room sizes. We can get a feel for traffic patterns. It makes the plan come alive. Also, by having had them send pictures, you kind of have an idea of what you're working with and what kind of lifestyle they have. If they have big comfy furniture, what does that tell you about their lifestyle versus something that's very sleek and modern? It will help you to better understand how to communicate to them based on their preferences.

Let's say you are a listing agent, and you're there trying to get that listing. Why can't you create homework for that customer as well? You know, send them to some different websites, to look at different homes on the market, show them what they should look for. Go ahead and teach them how to do some comparisons. Same thing with resale markets. If you're showing resale homes, why not send them to certain websites? I know they all get on them themselves. Every realtor I talked to says, "Oh gosh, they already send me 20 different houses they want to see all over town, and they won't let me do my job." But once you've shown them a few they realize they're not as good at picking a home for themselves as you are, because you're the expert and the professional.

Maybe you can send them to some different options, and you can share with them some things they should look at. So, our first point is give them homework. Then my closing tool is, it will take me a couple of days to pull all this together. And now we go with alternative choices. I'm going to say for example, "Would a weekend be better? Or are mornings better or afternoons better." You all know the alternative choice tactic that's been out there for forever. This is how we use it now by showing them what we're going to do. It's something fun and they don't feel like they're being closed on. They are more likely to set an appointment with you.

The other piece of this? I see a lot of people trying to set an appointment by saying, "When would you like to come back in?" Think of all the hours in the day for all the weeks and months ahead and come up with one time that works. You know what they'll say every time? They have to go home and check their schedule; I'll let you know. And now we're back in phone follow-up mode because they're not really quick to get back to us with a date and time.

But if you'll make alternative choices and say Monday or Tuesday, weekday or weekend, morning or afternoon, and then you propose a time you'll have more success. A little tip here, propose a time on the quarter hour. Why? Because if you pose the time on the hour, like three o'clock, it sounds very arbitrary. It also tends to make them feel like they're for sure going to be stuck with you for an hour. Instead suggest 3:15. Then they may think the appointment might only take 45 minutes at the most. If I say 3:30, it's a half an hour. That's how people mentally look at timeframes.

Always tell them you have two openings. "I have the afternoon on Thursday. I have 3:15, or I have Friday at 2:45. What works better for you?" Don't ask them to tell you what time they would like to come on any given day. If you let them pick the time, it says something else to them. I have no business. I'm free every minute of the day, come on down anytime and have an appointment with me. Do people want to buy from people they don't think are successful? No. So if you look busy and you suggest times, they believe you're busy. They believe you have other people coming in, and it creates urgency. Every one of you wants to know how to create urgency. Well, when your time isn't free and you're limited on accessibility, what does that say? I'm busy. If you're busy, then that must mean you're selling. And if you're selling, what mindset does that create for the potential buyer? "I want to get on the bandwagon and work with somebody that's successful."

What do you do if you can't get the next appointment while you're with them? Maybe you feel, "I didn't really do a great demonstration. I really didn't get to that place where I knew what I wanted to say to them so that I could get them to come back in." And then you made the historic mistake of saying, "When would you like to come back in?"

And they said, "I'll get back to you."

We all have good days and bad days, I do too. There are days when it just doesn't all come together. So, what do you do" Go back and review the conversation you had with them and see what things they need to know that were not addressed. Remember we talked earlier on in one of the very first chapters about the need for answering questions that are required for that prospect to make a decision. Things like, "Why would I want to buy this home versus the competition?" Or "Why would I want to buy in this area? Why would I want to buy in this neighborhood? Why would I want to work with this sales professional?" Remember, when you start refreshing your mind on the conversation that you had, one of those areas will stick out and that becomes the reason for your next call.

For example, let's say we didn't talk about the neighborhood they wanted to live in. I might make the call and say, "Hi, Mr. and Mrs. Jones, I just wanted to get back in touch with you. I was thinking about you last night." By the way I always say that I was thinking about them either this morning or last night, that they were on my mind because people want to believe they're important to you, especially if you're trying to sell them anything. Again I would say, "I was thinking about you last night and about the conversation we had, and I realized I don't really know what's most important to you about the aspects of the neighborhood you see yourself living in. We didn't talk about that. Would you mind sharing with me some of the things that are most important to you about the neighborhood you'd like to be in now?" If I'm a new home salesperson, I'm in the neighborhood. So when I know what they want, I can invite them to come back out and show them the things I did not show them before that now meet their needs. If I am a realtor, trying to get them into a specific home, maybe this gives me more ideas of things that I can pull up that are a better fit neighborhood wise than what I did before.

Always go to those questions and see what you didn't cover, because those questions are really the purpose for the next appointment. That way you can cover the issues that were not addressed, and you can help them get the answers that they need. Remember, never make them feel like the purpose of the appointment is to buy. That is the quickest way of not getting an appointment. They do not want to feel pressure. They don't want to feel like they're being roped into something. So, this is so incredibly important to remember that we're just trying to get them information.

Alright, so now let's say we have to do some follow-up and where are we going to use one of four different ways. There's email, a phone call, text and video. Let's start with the phone call, which many of us Baby Boomers learned was the only way to follow up in the sales process. We've talked about multiple generational conversations and we now know a phone call isn't for everyone. Right?

Most people, when they make a phone call to follow up are horrified because they don't have a planned script. I don't usually teach the use of scripts, but I'm going to advocate it here. I want you to write your own. Every script is specific for every person you're going to call. If you don't have that script and you get voicemail, you might start rambling on and give too much information and you never get a phone call back. So, let's talk about scripting for a minute. I saw this in my own business years ago, I was working as a consultant, working with different builders. I knew so many of these different individuals from having worked with them at the home builders association when I was president. So, I knew people and I knew that they knew who I was, and I believed that they would probably value my call.

So, I went to make a call to set up an appointment, to visit with one of these builders. And it was one of those deals where at the end, the prompt came up. Would you like to review your message? Okay. I'm going to review my message. I was appalled. Oh my gosh, I present for a living. I train for a living. I teach for a living. I speak for living. And yet, if you'd have heard me on that call, you would have said, "What are you thinking about your profession and your career now?" You're an idiot. I felt like I had all sorts of different things I was saying in my message. I wasn't coherent. I realized I should delete it now and get off the phone. And it was at that point in time, I decided that if I wanted to create a compelling message, I needed to write it out beforehand.

Now most people in sales think the reason they're so good at sales is they can fly by the seat of their pants. Sure, in a sales presentation, you have to watch for different reactions from people. You may have to shift gears. But I'm telling you when you're leaving a message on voicemail, that's not the time to fly by the seat of your pants. All it will do is make you crash and burn. So, when you're going to make a phone call, you want to be prepared for the voicemail, because nine times out of 10, you get one chance so make sure it's short and sweet. It needs to be less than a minute long. It needs to be scripted. You need to hit the points fast and furious.

For example, I had a salesperson I was working with. Let's call her Sherry. Sherry told me that she tried calling up somebody and she didn't understand why they didn't return her call. I said, "Well, what was the purpose of your call?" In this particular situation, she had done some pricing of some decorator items that the person wanted to have built into their home. So, she called them up. She got their voicemail, and she left all the pricing information for them on the voicemail. Now I'm sure as you're reading this, you're thinking she shouldn't have done that. Exactly. Sherry gave them all the information they needed. Now, there is no point for them to call Sherry back until it meets their needs to call her back.

When you're going to leave messages, make sure it's a compelling message. One that compels the person to want to call you back. Sherry should have left this message, "Mr. and Mrs. Smith, this is Sherry with XYZ builder. I wanted to get back to you. I was working on your pricing, and I had a question about something that I was unsure of. Could you give me a call at your earliest possible convenience so I can get this question answered and get the rest of your pricing done?" She later tried that, and you know what? She got a call back within 30 minutes because now they felt like they couldn't get the information without that phone call. And what she did is she asked a couple of questions about some things, even though she felt she had all the information and then created a strategy for them to come back out.

Here's something else I want to share with you. For those who do pricing, because you work with a builder, I implore you to not text, email or leave on voicemail, pricing for people. Now they have all the information they do not need you. And you're going to sit there waiting, waiting, and waiting on many of these people until they get back around to you.

By using that script and creating something actionable for the customer to respond to now there's something in it for them. It's not to try to sell them. It's to say, I want to make sure as we go over this and I'm showing you pictures, or I'm explaining it to you, or I'm drawing it out for you, we are absolutely on the same page for what you wanted me to price.

Last of all, I want to talk to you about something that makes most people laugh at me when I say it, but it is a technique I learned a long, long time ago. When I call people on the phone I'm smiling, because a smile actually can be heard. Just hear me out. What am I saying? When you get on that phone, have a mirror somewhere near you. I know it's a little off putting but pull that mirror out and speak into that mirror and look at yourself. When you're smiling, your voice has a very different tenor than when you're frowning or when there's no expression. This is so important these days with all the Zoom or WebEx meetings where people are seeing you face to face. But when we don't have anyone in front of us, it's really very hard to be compelling in the message and to make it feel like we're passionate about what we're talking about and that we're enjoying what we're doing, because we see no expression.

Let's talk about email. The very first thing you need to understand is the subject line is everything. A lot of times when I'm working with people I'll see them, if they're working for a builder, put something in the subject line about an update on ABC community. That's a good way to get deleted. If I'm a realtor and I say let's talk about listing your home. Deleted. I'm a realtor, I've got some homes you might want to look at. Deleted because the message is very boring. One of the things you can assure yourselves of is that in today's world, if you want to get an email read, make the subject line bold and in your face and make it look like they're losing something over it. Think about the news. There's an old adage that says, "If it bleeds, it leads." So many TV stations have tried to put up positive news first, but it didn't work. Everybody wants to see the gore, the violence, the bad news, whatever. I don't know what we get out of that intrinsically, but humans do get something out of that. It's like when you're driving down the street and there's an accident, what does everybody do? Even though it's three lanes over and your lane's not impacted. Maybe the accident is across the freeway. What does everybody do? They slow down because they want to see what happened. Well, it's the same with email. I've got to create a compelling subject line in order for me to get read.

Let's say I'm going to get a price increase. Instead of saying price increases coming from my neighborhood, delete, okay, I already know what you're saying. I don't really want to read what you have to say. If instead I said, "You're about to miss the best opportunity available." Guess what? Somebody's going to open that email. "I'm going to miss out on opportunity." Nobody wants to miss out on anything. You've heard that new acronym, FOMO, fear of missing out; it's real. So anytime you can craft a subject line that makes somebody feel like that. If they don't read the rest of the body of the email, they're going to be missing out. They're going to pay attention.

I had a salesperson that I was working with a couple of months ago. We'll call her Karen. She had a number of prospects that she couldn't get to respond back to her. So, she decided she would try something really funny. And what she did is say, "Are you tired of dating me already?" Let me tell you what, she works with a CRM system that allows you to see open rates. She got a 95% open rate. Basically, she said in her email, "If we're breaking up, someone at least tells me they don't want to hear from me anymore. Maybe you've already found a home. Maybe you've decided to put this on hold. Would you mind letting me know either way what your intentions are? I don't want to bother you anymore."

This may not be something you want to do, but she got a great open rate, right? And out of that open rate, she got about a 60% response rate. Some of them told her they'd already bought somewhere else. A lot of times when people don't respond, that is exactly what they've done. But she got a response. Right? What I would suggest you do is go to your own personal email and look at some of those subject lines that you end up opening.

Here's another example of the power of a great subject line in an email. Another salesperson I worked with, Natalie, was complaining that someone she thought was a really great prospect and ready to buy had now "ghosted" her (ghosted is a term many use when the prospect is receiving your emails, was interested in buying before, but now responds to no communication - like they had become a ghost). In her situation, she was very budget conscious and very particular about the lot she wanted. During the past week, another buyer had cancelled their contract on a lot this woman would like. In this situation, Natalie told me she was going to email this woman and let her know this lot was available. Not so fast!

Had Natalie given that information to her buyer, the buyer now has all the information and will respond when it comes to her time frame. Natalie was also concerned that maybe this buyer had bought somewhere else. See how these perceptions occur? Natalie's perception was that if this buyer were still interested, she would respond. So, Natalie's assumption was the buyer bought somewhere else and Natalie's initial choice was to stop contacting the buyer.

Instead, we crafted an email that started with the subject line of "There is a window of opportunity that is about to close on you." Then our body copy went on to say that over the past week a situation had arisen that had changed lot availability within the neighborhood. Natalie wanted to visit with the buyer to explain this situation before the window of opportunity closed, and the situation changed again. What happened? Natalie's prospect responded back within hours. Why had the buyer not responded before then? She had had dental surgery the past week and wasn't able to talk. Wow, far different from buying somewhere else, right?

Natalie told the buyer how a lot had come available because of the cancelled contract and let the buyer know other customers were looking at this lot and that time was of the essence. The result? The buyer came out, ended up staying on the original lot she liked and wrote a contract. From ghost to buyer in one simple email.

Number two, as I said before, if you're going to use a subject line that is sensationalism, you've got to refer back to it. So for example, if I said, "You're about to miss out on one of the biggest opportunities available," my body copy then needs to say, I wanted to get in touch with you, John and Judy, because we're going to be experiencing a price increase in the next 30 days (or the next week or whatever that is) that will actually take away the equity position you would have gained had you bought before this price increase. I didn't want you to miss out on this opportunity.

I've tied the two together. You can't put out a sensational topic and then not follow up in the body copy and show how it relates. Be short and to the point. I see emails that are five paragraphs long and there's like six and seven sentences in every paragraph. Nobody's going to read that. I can't tell you how many emails I started reading. Oh gosh, this looks interesting. I don't have time right now. And of course, my email box keeps filling up and filling up. And now those emails are three months old. And guess what? At some point in time, what do I do? I just dump it all and start all over again, which is what most people do. So, don't make your email five paragraphs long. Shouldn't be any more than three paragraphs. Your first paragraph should be some introduction that relates to your subject line.

Your body paragraph, or paragraph number two, should be like three or four bullet points that are very short, that express what you're trying to do. And then line three should be a call to action. Now, when I say call to action, I see something like "for more information on the impending price increase and what it will do for you contact me….." That's the softest, biggest snowball, that no one's ever going to answer, right? I want to say something that's very action oriented.

Here's an example of an action-oriented email. "The three biggest mistakes I see people most often make when buying a home are trying to buy based on price per square foot, trying to make a decision based on feature level and three, trying to buy a home based on incentives. If you'd like more information on why these three will actually get you into trouble, simply reply using the word INFORMATION. I will send you a short synopsis of why these three things are the biggest mistakes most people make when trying to buy a home." We get pretty big open rates on this and we get pretty good response rates on this.

I was working with one client and we put that email into production and it went out and I got a call from a salesperson, and he said, " I got a bunch of responses that said they wanted information." I said, "Wow, this is a great problem to have." We created a PDF document that we could send out and it was very successful for him. So, as I said, subject lines are everything, be short and to the point, use bullet points and place a call to action.

Now let's talk about texts. Everybody's texting these days. Now, we've learned we probably don't want to text a traditionalist. And if I'm really trying to get information to a client about housing, which is a big-ticket item, baby boomers aren't going to be my fans with texting either. If I want to get somebody to respond who is a Gen Xer by text, who really prefers email, I can get a response but it is tricky. Let me give you an example. A salesperson that I was working with had gone through this very seminar on talking to different generations. Let's call her Stacy. Stacy called me and said, "I don't know what to do here."

I said, "What do you mean?"

She said, "Well, these people text me questions and I respond back on text and I never get a response."

So I asked her, "Stacy, how old are these people?" We determined they were probably Gen Xers.

"Why don't you respond back to their texts via email?" She did and you know what? She got back a five paragraph, email response when they hadn't been responding to text at all.

So just remember, just because someone texts you doesn't mean that that's necessarily how they want you to respond. It's just an easy and fast way for them to blurt out their thoughts. When you text someone always use their first name, there's power in using someone's first name. What it says is when you reply with the first name, you actually know who's texting you. When you're working with customers it's probably a good idea to put them in your cell phone so when they do text you and the phone number comes up, you know who it is. Once you've finished with them, you can take them out of your database, but it's good to have them in there.

When they do text, think about audio messages. People are busy and let's say, they're driving, and we're not supposed to look at our phone when we're driving, and we get a text. What about leaving a short audio message instead of trying to respond to somebody, maybe make it interesting, use their first name and give them a short message back. Everyone likes to hear the sound of their name. And they also like to hear your voice giving them a short message.

Now, remember if you're going to use an audio message, it's got to be really short. I wouldn't recommend it to be any longer than 15 or 20 seconds. So, you might even say, "I got your text, not in a position to answer it at this moment, but I will get back with you shortly." That's a great way to do that.

Also, you have to be very succinct in a text. I read texts for people that go on for paragraphs. Do you ever get that? And doesn't it just infuriate you? When you're thinking, why didn't you just call me? In fact, I did that the other day with one of my clients. We had a very difficult issue that was going on. He texted me back and said, "This is stupid texting back and forth." We both agreed it was just better to use the phone. So be very succinct. If you can't be succinct, then you probably need to resort to a phone call or to an email.

WARNING......never become a text stalker! What does that mean? I'm sure some of you are like, "Oh God, how did she know I do that?" I watch salespeople become dateless and desperate, that's what I call it when they have no sale for the month. They thought they were going to sell a few homes. There's nothing on the horizon. They had one good prospect they thought was going to do something. They haven't done anything yet. They text, they don't hear anything back. And all of a sudden, they text again, like 30 minutes later. They don't hear anything. They give them an hour. They text them. If you're texting someone five, six, seven times a day, stop, just don't do it. What that says is, my favorite line, you're dateless and desperate. What it tells that person is I have no other clients. You're the only one on the hook.

What's the expectation when you're texting? The expectation is you're going to hear back immediately. This is a frustration I see in this business altogether. When people text, they expect they should hear from you immediately. I got to admit I'm the same way. If I text somebody with a quick question, and then I haven't heard from them for two or three hours, I start wondering if they got the text or if they're just dissing me. Well, same thing with your customer. If you text them as a communication and then don't respond to their texts for two or three hours, what you're saying is you're very disorganized and you're not very thoughtful of people's time. So never text if you can't respond quickly.

One of the most effective things we now have in today's world and has become more and more valuable is video. As I'm writing this book, we're just in the throes of coming out of the second wave of the coronavirus pandemic. Many of you have lived in places or experienced the fact that you were required to wear a mask in a social setting situation, especially in a real estate transaction. Unfortunately, when people wear masks, you can never see their full face. You see their eyes, but you don't know what they really look like. You never saw a smile. Smiles. When I teach people how to build a relationship, one of the very first things I've always taught is to smile immediately upon seeing someone. Smiles absolutely break down barriers. Now we don't have that available to us. So, videos have become a great way to follow-up with customers.

I have a salesperson named Susanna. She said, "You know, I just feel bad because I don't get to smile, and people don't see my smile. I don't see their smile." So, we came up with the idea of doing a video. It's a follow-up video that was only 15 seconds long. This is the face behind the mask. She did a very cute little video saying, "It was so nice of you to come in. It was such a pleasure meeting you. I just wanted you to see there is a whole face behind this mask. And I look forward to talking to you again." There was no business. There was no, "Let's set another appointment." There was none of those things. It was just a thank you. And in some of them, she may have referenced their children. Again, it was just a way of creating recognition and being memorable.

When you use video, you also have to use people's first names. You don't want a video that you're using as follow-up to look like it's the same video you've sent to 55 other customers. This is one important thing. When we talked about dollars being in the demonstration, the more personal information you know about people, the better off you are. So for example, if you happen to have somebody that works in your sales office on your days off or gets leads for you, ask them to get personal information, dogs' names, cats' names, kids' names, things they like, things they do so that when we do this, you can absolutely have a personalized video that says, "Hi, Deborah. It was such a pleasure visiting with you the other day. It was great to hear about your dog, Ziggy. And I'm sure you're really excited about your new puppy, Tilly. Jessica, thank you for your time. I look forward to talking to you again in the future." Think about it. Think about how that makes a person feel if the salesperson has used personal information to say thank you in a video, you think they're more likely to respond? Absolutely. Because now they feel indebted to a certain degree. They've got the go ahead to move forward and do something because they were kind enough to remember me.

As we started this chapter, it was about first setting an appointment while the people are there. If all "you know what" breaks loose and that's not possible, and you have to do follow up, then be thoughtful with your follow up.

ACTION PLAN:

- Really work to hone your appointment setting strategies for people while they're there. Remember we used alternate choice of dates, alternate choice of times, and then provide times that are on the quarter or half hours so that people feel like that the amount of time they're going to spend with you is relatively short versus being there with you for hours. If you didn't get the next appointment? Go to the next step.

- Go ahead and review what you know about that prospect against the different questions that you know they have to have mentally answered before they can make a buying decision. Make your appointment strategy all about helping them find answers to those questions.

- Work on your forms of follow up. Create a script. Before you make phone calls, think about your emails, create compelling, interesting subject lines, and really work on honing your skills at bullet pointing out prospective points you want someone to know. Make sure when you're doing a text that you use someone's first name. Try working on doing some short audio messages so that you get some that you like so you can use them more frequently. Make sure that you are always texting when you can respond quickly and lastly, work on some videos you can send out as reminders that will help you get that next appointment, or at least reconnect with someone. I can assure you that if you change your strategy, I'm pretty sure that you're going to see a huge difference in the appointments that you've set. And remember this, without appointments, sales usually don't get made.

CHAPTER SIX

Everyone Wants
to Negotiate

ARE YOU READY? I would say that many of the sales professionals I work with are most disturbed and most worried about negotiation. I read a book some time ago about negotiation and it said, "Really great negotiators are the ones who don't have anything to lose in the negotiation."

Wow. Think about that. "Really great negotiators are the ones that don't have anything to lose in the negotiation." I don't know who has more to lose than a sales professional when the negotiation goes south. If a deal isn't made, and most of you are on commission, you don't get paid. Negotiation is probably one of the most challenging things that you have to do in any kind of transaction. There is fear that if the negotiation doesn't work out, you will lose your opportunity to make a sale. It's a different scenario when you are negotiating something on behalf of somebody; you'll get paid no matter what. The same thing goes when you are a new home sales professional, and you have a sales manager. Your manager will still get their check even though the negotiation went south.

It's scary because most sales professionals I know have had very little experience or training in negotiation. They always ask what are the best ways to negotiate? How do I do it? What are the techniques that I should use, and how do I make it work? That's what we're going to talk about. The first thing I want to tell you is that most people go wrong with negotiation because they treat it as an event and not a process. Think about that. They treat negotiation as an event and not a process. You see, negotiation is always a process. It is also a game. In fact, most negotiation strategies that are out there today are all based on game theory.

Game theory is a theoretical framework utilized in business and economics. This framework helps us to understand how competing players (here the buyer and the seller) meet their goal of maximizing gains and minimizing losses in a situation where there are a finite number of outcomes. Now, most of you have probably heard that the best outcomes in negotiation are win-win. Game theory indicates that every negotiation is not necessarily win-win, where each side comes out equal. Winning is really about perception. Remember that little word we talked about in Chapter One, mindset? Mindset is about perception, and perception is how you look at things. Did both parties walk away thinking they got a fair deal? I didn't say the perfect deal. I didn't say I have everything they wanted. Did they feel like it was fair? If you and the customer can walk away from a negotiation feeling like it was fair, then probably you're going to get the deal done.

Negotiation is also predicated by a few other things: people's personality styles, their upbringing, and their training. So, let's go from the bottom up here. Think about it. If you're working with a manager, do you think that maybe his company may have sent him to negotiation classes? You're right, his company probably has. Some of the customers we work with actually are much better experts at negotiation than we are because we've never learned the basic tenets of negotiation. It is always important to understand what kind of background they have - did they attend formal training? Because if they did, you should prepare for some tricks of negotiation hidden in their sleeves.

A lot of people were raised in a culture where negotiation is revered as a personality trait. How good a negotiator you are is a status symbol. However, most of us didn't grow up having this trait, or even learning how to gain it. I would guess that most of you haven't gone into the grocery store contemplating this outcome. You go to buy eggs and when you open the carton you find one egg is cracked, so you tell the saleslady that you're only going to buy the carton of eggs if she gives a 50 cent discount. Most of us were never taught to negotiate like this, but based on some cultures, there are people who do that every day, and I think we should take a lesson from that. Indeed, what's the point of getting the whole dozen and paying the exact amount when maybe you can get a discount because of the cracked egg?

Do you understand how vital negotiation is? As a sales professional, you can't just go ahead and say, "I'm just not playing that game. The price is the price. Here's what it is. If you want to negotiate, I'm not your person." What you really just said translates to, "I don't care that you're different from me. I don't care that you see the world differently. I'm just going to go ahead and make you do it my way."

My friends, that's not what we teach in sales. Everything that we've been talking about in this book so far has been about understanding how customers communicate. It's about understanding their values and their needs, wants, and desires, even their perception and attitude. And yet when it comes down to negotiating a price on a property, we're going to say that we're not playing their game because WE don't like it?

Most of the time, people take this stance because they don't know how to negotiate. They're scared. It is scary because you know at some point in time you may actually have to say, "This is the number, take it or leave it." Sometimes that's hard to do, right? Then we have personality styles. You know, some people are hard bargain negotiators, they're driver personalities. They want to be the bull in the china shop. They're going to make this happen at their price. And then you have other people who might say to you, "Is there any negotiation on the price?" And you say, "No, not really." They will say, "Oh, okay, well, I just had to ask." So, we really have to understand personality styles as well, which will also indicate how individuals are going to negotiate.

Now let's talk about some cool negotiation tactics, the how-to's of negotiation. The first thing I will talk about is an anchor. What comes to your mind? What if I ask you to visualize a boat anchor? What is it, and how is it used? An anchor is used to keep the boat in a specific spot. Basically, it's anchored to that spot.

Well, one of the most effective tools of negotiation is the creation of the anchor. As I mentioned earlier, negotiation is a process, not an event. Let's talk about how the anchor starts the process for us. I don't care if you're a realtor or a new home salesperson, every time a prospect comes to you, they're going to tell you how much their budget is, am I right? They will say, "We're looking at houses in the $350,000 price point" or "We're looking at homes in the $500,000 price point." Or they may come in and say, "I've only been qualified up to $500,000." Or "I've only been qualified up to $150,000." That is an anchor. They're trying to put a figure out there that sets the bottom range of the negotiation.

Now, for those of you who are new home salespeople, you have a price list. I know so many people get frustrated because the customer walks in and says, "Well, we're looking at a house around $300,000 - $350,000," and your lowest price starts at $375,000. The very first thing you want to say is, "I don't have anything that can help you," but you shouldn't do that. Many of you try to mitigate the distance between your price and what the buyer has given you by giving away incentive money. Again, not the best plan! So, let's say they want a home at $350k. Your prices start at $365k. You have $10,000 worth of incentive. Here's what I see happen all the time. Well, my price has started at $365k, but I can take $10,000 off the price. So, I can actually start at $350,000.

Now here's the key ingredient. Do you think anyone really believes that whatever you offer up so quickly is all that you can give them? Do you really think they believe that's all they're going to get? The answer is no. And that's why they come back and ask you for more. Salespeople tell me all the time, "I gave them my incentive. Now they want more." Well, of course, they did. No one thinks in the real world, everybody's going to put all their cards on the table so quickly. They believe they are only going to put a few cards down, so they have the rest of the hand to play with. You have to understand, that's the effect of the anchor. So, every time you are to be involved in a negotiation, set your anchor first.

Okay, think about it this way. If a customer comes in and says, I'm looking for a home at $350,000, and you start at $365,000, they set the anchor where you feel like you have to minimize that distance. Now what happens if they walk in the door and you say, "You know, most people that come in here can afford anything that we have to offer. So, I just would like to share with you that our prices start at $365,000 and go up to blah, blah, blah." See, now what you've done is you set the anchor, you set the arbitrary anchor as negotiations go along.

There is a falsehood that has been propagated for a long time in real estate that says, "Try to get the buyer to make the offer first." Think about that. Try to get the buyer to make the offer. So, if we're talking about anchors, who just set the anchor? The buyer. And what's a smart buyer going to do? They're going to try to set that anchor arbitrarily low so that you're forced to have to give up as much money as you can, as quickly as you can.

Game theory tells us that the person most likely to win the game is the one who makes the first offer, not vice versa. So, if you really want to be the one to get to where you need to go, you've got to set the anchor first. Think about that. You set the anchor first. Now what happens? The buyer is in the position you once were in trying to minimize that distance. And now you keep them from coming in with a low-ball offer.

Here's what I mean when I reference low-ball offers. Let's say your house is priced at $375,000, and the buyer comes in and offers $325,000. You might say, "There's no way I can make that work at

$325,000. We'll see what we can do." So you come back and you give them some kind of counter, in the range of $355,000 to $360,000 and they say, "Oh gosh, well that's just too much. But we can bring our offer up to $340,000." They look for another counter. And perhaps you come to $355,000 or even $350,000, and then they bring out their very favorite trick. They say, "You would lose a sale over $10,000? I can't believe your company would lose a sale over $10,000." Some salespeople then propose to split the difference. Well, there's a book called *Never Split the Difference* by Chris Voss. Voss explains how the one who initially says let's split the difference will always end up paying more than the person who agreed to split the difference. What does that mean? So, let's say they're at $350,000 and I'm at $360,000. We have a $10,000 difference. And I say, "Okay, let's split the difference. Let's do it." That's $355,000.

"Oh gosh. Well, I can't do $355,000. I could go up to $353,000."

And you go, "Well, we need to make it $355,000."

And then again, they continue with, "You would lose a sale over $2,000?" And now we're running back to our seller, to our manager, to whomever it is, repeating the question "we would lose the sale over $2,000?"

Perhaps we get lucky and the decision-maker agrees to lower the price to hit the buyer's number. And so, guess what? They still got away with less than we did. That's what the difference is now. Instead of just a $5,000 difference it became a $7,500 difference for us and only $2,000 difference for them. That's why it never works. Never meet their price. It's based on the psychology that if it's too easy to get, I didn't work hard enough to get it.

I had a client the other day who had a customer come in and say, "I know the house is listed at $400,000, but if you can sell it to us for $385,000, we'll sign on the dotted line and we'll get you the earnest money. We'll buy the house today." Sales professionals think, "Great. This is awesome. I have a sale." She calls her manager. "Can we get this house down to $385,000? Because these people said, ``If I can get to that number, they will absolutely buy today."

The manager runs all the numbers and says, "Yes, we can make that happen."

The sales professional picks up the phone, says "Mr. or Mrs. customer, guess what? I've got such great news for you. I'm able to sell you that house at $385,000. When can you come in and sign the paperwork?' And this invariably is the answer. "Well, we were talking about it after we called you. I did say we would buy it today for $385,000, but we really looked at some additional comps in the neighborhood. And we really think that's maybe overpaying a little. We only want to pay $380,000. Can you get that done?" Or they may say, "We were talking, and I appreciate that you can get it to $385,000, but we really need blinds in the house. So, can you throw that in?"

When the sales professional goes back and talks to somebody and can so easily meet the buyer's request and says, "Guess what? Good news. I was able to make it happen." The customer feels like they left money on the table. And that's the biggest challenge for most buyers today. They don't want to leave money on the table. So how do they know when that happens? Unfortunately, the only way they know is when you say, "No." Interestingly enough, as an aside, I think what we all have to realize is that we don't like to negotiate because for most of us, our most recent experience with negotiation is buying cars. Most people feel like they never really got a good deal. They really didn't understand what they were buying the new car for based on the trade in, or they really never knew what the trade in value was based on the new car. As a result, they just always felt like it was push, push, push, and then the dealer said, "No," and then they start walking out the door and then the dealer comes back and says, "Wait, I'll make it happen." People have had a bad experience with negotiation and just felt like they got taken advantage of; they bring those experiences to the table with us, we have to remember that. Of course the buyer wants to know that they bought this house for the best price possible and did not overpay at some point in time, but again, never meet their price.

What I might say to somebody is, "Oh gosh, I fought and fought and fought with my manager. I wasn't able to get you 385, but I was able to get 386,123." Now, if you're paying attention, what did I do? I came in with a really odd ball number. Very interesting, right? The mind perceives that if the number is odd and I don't mean like an odd number in that it ends in three, five, an odd number, it's just not a rounded number, it appears that somebody actually put a pencil to paper to try to figure out what the best deal possible was.

Most of us in negotiations, if the house they wanted is at 385, we go, "Well, I can sell it at 385-five, or 381-five." That number sounds contrived. It doesn't sound like anybody tried really hard to give them the best deal possible. So, when you come in with the number that's very odd and they think pencil went to paper and everybody's working in their best interest to try to get them what they want, it's easier to get the customer to your number. I would say, "I worked really hard to get there, and I couldn't quite get it. The best I could do is $381,123." Now, if a buyer is not going to buy a house over $1,123, were they really a buyer in the first place? I'm not talking about whether they qualify for the extra $1,100? That's a whole different topic in itself, but let's assume they can qualify for this, are you really going to lose a sale over $1,100? Probably not.

Unless you get into a great market, where we actually have people paying above market value because there's a shortage of homes on the market, you need a strategy. What's your strategy? To determine that my first question is, "What do you think their offer is going to be?" I can't tell you how many times I hear somebody say, "I have no idea." Well, then we cannot create a strategy if you don't know where they're going to come in. How would you find that out? Very simple. The buyer might say, "Well, we're going to be making you an offer." Your response should be, "Could you kind of give me a range of where you think you're going to be making this offer, because I really don't want to waste your time having you come in and write an offer that would never have a chance of never being accepted." What if we're not even in the same ballpark? Most people can give you a number, right? If I'm going to play with the strategy, the way I've taught you to play it, I would basically say, "If you're going to be coming in with an offer, I can tell you the best I'm going to be able to accept is…" Set the anchor. It doesn't mean you won't go any lower than that, but set the anchor. Now they're going to have to work up closer to it. Otherwise they start arbitrarily low. Clients like to tell you how much they've come up on their offer. But what they came up to on their offer wasn't really valuable because the initial offer was so extremely low!

The third part of the strategy is, if I'm going to give anything, I need to get something. This is called the string in negotiation. Remember if you give somebody a price, a lowered price, and don't ask them to do something in return for that lowered price, they see no value in the accommodation you've made. We don't want to do that. We want them to see that what we've done is really in their best interests. So, what are my strategies? Well, first of all, when I have a certain amount of dollars to give away, I use what I call the five volleys. My first offer to the customer is going to be 70% of what I can give away. And then I do smaller and smaller amounts until I've gone back to them five times.

Now, what does that do? First of all, they see that number getting smaller and smaller and smaller, which tells them they are taking all the money off the table. But number two, I asked for something in return. So, for example, I might say the very first anchor setting offer I make is a freebie. I give the customer a discount off the price right off the bat. But let's say the customer comes back and says, "That's not good enough."

And we say, "Well, I could do this, if you could close earlier than what you said," because if I'm working for a builder, I might indicate that I am giving the customer that amount because my builder is going to save that much in interim interest with an earlier closing. In addition, I'm going to save the builder the cost of electricity, heating, maintenance, watering the lawns, cleaning the house, whatever all goes into that number. If it's for a seller and I'm a realtor, it could be by closing earlier, we can minimize the additional taxes paid, whatever it may be.

I can ask the buyer to loan apply sooner rather than later, even you realtors have people with pre-qualification letters. They haven't necessarily loan applied. They've just called somebody up and said, "Hey, can I qualify for $325,000?" They run some basic numbers and ask them what their credit score is. A lot of them haven't even pulled their credit score and they tell the buyer, "Yeah, you should be able to qualify for this." So maybe as a realtor or as a builder, I would say, "You know, I can take some additional money off if we can get a loan application completed in one day instead of five days, okay." I could say that I can give additional money off or I might be able to negotiate additional monies off the house because it indicates to the seller that this buyer is acting in good faith.

That works with giving more earnest money as well. I can tell the buyer, "If you'll give me more earnest money, it just shows the seller that you're really, really motivated to buy this house." This is just a game we're playing. So, do you see, you can make all these things up. If I'm a builder, I could be doing something where I would say if they got into the design center and made their selections earlier, I could do something on price. You just have to be creative and think about it. But if you're going to lower the price, remember there is no value for the discount you just gave if they didn't have to do something to get it.

One salesperson that I was working with, Tiffany, told me that when she utilized this process with buyers, it only took about two or three volleys and they were done. They figured out that they were going to have to go ahead and give something up in order to get more off the price. They got tired of the process and they stopped.

Another strategy you can use if you are a builder and you are going to build a home for somebody, you can use the Three Options strategy. With this strategy I am going to price out the home three different ways. First I am going to give the buyer a price that gets as close to their budget number and include any options, if possible, that they wanted in that number. The second option includes the base price and some additional extras they wanted. The third option will be the base price and everything they wanted included. When I provide the buyer with these three different scenarios, not only do I give them the three scenarios based on price, but also monthly payment. That is always a great thing to use as a negotiation strategy, because unless the buyer's a cash buyer, they're making monthly payments. And so many people get fixated on price, but truly what the buyer is paying for the house each month is what really matters. It also reduces the pricing down to a more manageable number. Let's say the difference between the second and third option is $20,000. Perhaps that equates to about $90 per month. $90 a month sounds way more manageable than $20,000, right?

I think many sales professionals stay away from this because we all say I'm not a mortgage lender. Your mortgage lender will be more than happy to show you how to figure out a monthly payment or calculate for you three different scenarios so that you can show people the difference per month. Why are we arguing over this $120 or $80 or $50 a month with our buyer? It's a no brainer once the buyer sees what it costs per month.

I'll give you the example. My husband bought a truck two years ago and we were sitting there and it's funny that I had to teach the car dealership finance guy, how to do this! We talked about it and he wanted to offer my husband an extended warranty. My husband takes great care of his vehicles, but he drives them a long time. So, the financial guy said, "Well, I could give you an extended warranty, but you know that that's going to cost you about $2,100?"

And I said, "No, it's not going to cost me $2,100."

He said, "Yeah, it is."

And I said, "No, it's not."

So, he finally asks me, "What are you talking about?"

I said, "We're not buying this car cash. We're buying it on monthly payments. So, what does that mean in the monthly payments?" I don't even know what the number was, but let's say it was $10. Well, $10 a month to have an extended warranty for a hundred thousand miles has value. When my husband puts a lot of miles on a truck that was a no brainer. Now I might not have wanted to give him a check for $2,100 or $2,500 or whatever it was, but $10 a month, I could certainly make that happen.

So just remember it's about the monthly payment, unless they're a cash buyer. That's what it's all about. What am I going to have to budget every month for that house? These are some of the strategies you can use when you're negotiating.

Now let me address something else. Negotiation is always easiest when you have leverage. What does that mean? Well, when you know somebody loves the house and they need to have it, you now have leverage; most of the time, the leverage is in the court of the buyer because you really don't know that they love your house the best.

Here are a couple of really cool things you should remember. Those of you in new home sales, when a buyer comes in and says, "I went over to builder XYZ, and they committed to selling me this house at X price, and I really love your house better. But if you can't meet that price, I'm going to go over and buy from them."

Now, pay attention because this is the interesting fact. People negotiate first with the person they least want to buy from, because they want to use that as leverage. When I come into your office and say, "XYZ builder is prepared to sell me that house today at this price. And if you don't meet or beat that price, I'm going to go over and buy from them," you believe that's the truth. And suddenly, you are the one trying to meet or beat that price. Let me tell you something. If they went to that length to get that leverage to use against you, they love your house best. You have the leverage. You have the ability to say "No."

Now a lot of my friends in this business would say "Wow, that is a great deal. Why didn't you buy it?" You never win in negotiation by insulting the other party. And I'll just say, that's pretty much an insult. It's pretty much a push. And when you push somebody, they push back. That's not a way to win a negotiation.

So many sales professionals have called me with the offer the buyer made, and they'll say, "Well, this is what they're offering, but I got to tell you, let's just let them sit for a day. I know they really want that house. They'll come back." You know that you have power in the negotiation. If they don't love your house, you can't win in the negotiation.

Interestingly enough, if they come to you first and they say, "I'm looking at another house over at XYZ builder, I need to know what you can do, because if they can beat that deal, I'm going to buy from them. But I'm going to give you your first shot." They don't like you best. My response in that situation is "If you're going to negotiate with me first, I know people don't negotiate first with the ones they liked the most. So, what is it about my house you don't like? That will certainly turn the tables on somebody for sure in that case. So always, always, always have a strategy. Know what leverage you have and know how emotionally involved they are. If they're emotionally involved in the house, they're going to come back.

For example, this just happened this weekend. I was working with a salesperson who had a buyer come in and the house had already been discounted. It was a builder home and had been on the market for longer than the builder wanted it to be. And so, this buyer came in with a really, really low offer.

There's no way this builder was going to take the offer. It would cause them to lose money. And that's just not a smart thing in real estate today. So, we worked on this together and the builder came back and told the sales professional that they had a counter, and they gave her the counter number. Well, the sales professional let the buyer sit all day long without a call. Her office closes at 6:00 pm and at 6:02 pm the realtor for the buyer calls saying, "Well, I haven't heard from you all day." They told the sales professional they were going to buy a house from another builder. Well, we knew that wasn't true. And later the realtor for the buyer came back to her and said, "Well, has your company decided to change their counter?"

And she said, "No."

They said, "Okay, well, we'll come up to this number," which was actually about $4,000 short of the counter that the builder had made. "Come up to this number, and we'll get everything done today," the buyer said.

The sales professional said, "Well, it's Labor Day." And she said, "I'm not going to get an answer today. So, if you really want to do this, then what you're going to need to do is make your offer the counter that my company gave you." And guess what happened? They told her they would get back with her in an hour and they did. They paid the builder's price. Now this client was pretty savvy. They played hard ball. They let the sales professional sit all day thinking, are they going to buy? Are they not going to buy? She wants the sale, but she and I have talked. And she realized that if she makes the call first, she's not going to get to where she needs to go. She also agreed that the price that we were asking the buyer to pay was more than fair. She knew she had the leverage because they were negotiating with her second, not first. And as a result, she won the day. That's how easy it can be.

What do I do when they come in with a low-ball offer? Well, the first thing I would do is use a physical reaction. When they come in with the low-ball offer and they're in front of you, flinch. Make them see that that was way unexpected. As I said before, never accept the first offer. But let's talk about some lines you can use that make people think about their offer differently. I might look at them and say, "Is that the best you can do?" Then be quiet. Don't say anything. The pressure is on them when silence occurs. Now, what I can also say to someone if it's a really low offer is, "We have had other offers that have come in that are higher than what you're prepared to offer. And those offers were rejected, but I'm still prepared to present your offer. However, in order to do that, I will need to understand your thoughts and the data you have that makes this offer reasonable."

For those of you in new home sales, just know, unless your managers ask you to present all offers, we're not required to present all offers. For my realtor friends, you are required to present all offers. In the scenario I just gave, I never told the buyer how much the other offer was. I never gave anything away, but I did let them know that probably that offer wasn't going to get them very far. Remember no negotiation is ever completely closed. There's always a way to reopen the door.

So, the last piece of this, and the hardest one I think I've ever had to work with, is the hot potato. The hot potato negotiation starts with "This is just not what we budgeted for." Now. I find this really interesting, right? They're looking at a house that is above their budget, and yet, in order to give them what they want, I am supposed to take a loss. If I'm a seller, whether I'm selling a resale or I'm selling a new home, I'm the one that's supposed to take the loss. They can have what they want because they didn't budget for more. Wow! That's when I look back at them and I say, "You didn't have a budget for that. Gosh, I'm confused as to why we were looking at this house when this house was never in the budget that you were looking for."

Notice, I didn't say that in a smart way. I didn't say it with tone. I didn't say it with that attitude. I just asked a question. Still, above all things you have to know when you'll have to walk away, you know, the old Kenny Rogers song, *The Gambler*, "You gotta know when to hold 'em, know when to fold 'em" in our business. Whether we're counseling a seller as a realtor or working with our boss trying to look at a deal, if at some point in time, the deal makes no sense, we have to tell that person. I would approach it this way, starting with, "Thank you so very much for your generous offer."

Now, you're probably thinking as you read that, why would I say it's generous? It was really low. I just want to be thankful and gracious that they even gave me a chance by offering something by saying, "Thank you for your generous offer. Unfortunately, we're not able to accept that price for this home at this time." And then be quiet. If you'll use some of these strategies, and if you really put them into play, you'll see negotiation is a process. It is not a one-off event. It is just the hurdle we have to get over in order to make that sale. And actually, the better you get at it the more fun you can have with it, because it actually can be your friend.

ACTION PLAN:

- When you're working with somebody, try to ascertain what kind of negotiation style they're going to have. Is it going to be predicated by customs they're used to? Is it going to be predicated by their personality or is it going to be predicated by training?

- Please re-read all of this information about anchors and leverage so that you can learn how to effectively use this in your presentation. I've given you a number of different examples, but as I've said before, not every example fits every personality. Find the ones that you think that you can work with and employ those. As a side note, if you know your seller needs more than what the buyer's asking for, what they need, you don't know enough about your buyer. Let me restate that. If you were working to negotiate a deal with your seller, whether that's your boss or actual homeowner, and you're trying to sell them on taking the deal because you have better leverage on them than you do on the customer, you don't know enough about the customer and you're now negotiating at the wrong point. You have to have the information to know how emotionally attached they are so you can have leverage.

- Always remember how people negotiate. Know when to walk away and know what to get in response to what you've given them in value. Remember, if you give a lower price and you haven't asked for something in return, what you gave them has absolutely no value.

CHAPTER SEVEN

Questions and Objections Are Your Best Friends

SOMEONE TOLD ME a long time ago (and they were very astute about this) that if no one ever asks questions about what you're saying, or objects to anything you're selling, they're really not interested. Think about that for a minute. If there's something that you want to buy and you like it, most of us kind of go, "Well, should I pay that much? Is that really the best color? Can I really use that?" Whenever we make a substantial purchase like buying a home, most of us list down all the objectives we have before we go ahead and drop that money down.

That's why I'm telling you that questions and objections are your best friends. If they don't question what you're selling, they have no questions or objections about what you're doing, they're probably not going to buy. I'll give you an example.

One of the sales professionals I was working with, Mary Jane, told me, "Oh gosh, I just don't understand why these people didn't buy."

I said, "Well, tell me the story."

And she said, "Oh, well, they came in, they loved my model. They loved all of the upgrades we had in it. We had a great conversation. I went ahead and showed them a lot we could build the home on. They loved that. They loved my price. They loved everything. And yet when it was all said and done, I said, "Well, if you love it, maybe we should just buy it." The prospects said they really loved it, but they needed to think about it more and that they would call her in the morning.

What happened? We all know the answer to this. The next morning came, there was no call. She tried to call them. She tried to email them. No response. Nothing happened. So, I explained to Mary Jane that somebody who loves everything about something she's offering and never once questioned her about it, was not really buying anything. We all know that. They've just gone along and made her feel good. In short, wasted her time.

That's why I tell you that it's crucial that people question you every time you make a pitch. Questions and objections asked are awesome. They are asking questions because they are interested, and they are trying to find out how it fits them or if it's for them. So, your role is to help them find the answer or solution. One of the things I want you to understand about working with questions and objections is that you need to be truly curious. A lot of people in this business aren't curious. They don't really want to know why somebody said something. They don't really want to know what's behind what someone says. And if you're going to be very, very successful in selling anything, you've got to be curious.

Every time someone says something to you, you need to say to yourself, "Why did they say that? Why did they describe it that way?

Why did they look at that answer from that perspective?" There's always something that is lurking behind their actions and statements. And if we can figure out what it is behind that question or objection, that curiosity will get us to the end game faster. Now, if I am curious, the question becomes, what questions do I ask? How do I find out what's lurking behind that question or objection that my prospect just gave me? Well, I read a book once called *Socratic Questioning*, and it helped me a lot up to now. So, what does Socratic questioning mean? Many of you know who Socrates was. He was a scholar and philosopher in Greek times.

Socrates taught his students by asking them question after question. This questioning process exposed the underlying thoughts and ideas of the students. Socrates then utilized his understanding of these thoughts and ideas to help the student form a definite conclusion. Notice, Socrates knew what the conclusion needed to be, but instead of telling it to his students, he questioned them into reasoning the same. It is so much more powerful for someone to believe they found the solution to their problem rather than being given the solution. So, I encourage people to utilize Socratic questions. What are those? They are questions that require the person answering to self-reflect. What does that really mean? It is asking a question in a way that requires your prospect to give you more than a yes or no answer.

Now I'm sure you're all thinking, "I've already learned that in sales training, that's called an open-ended question." Well, unfortunately, somewhere along the line, maybe 30, 40 years ago, some sales trainer in sales got the idea that an open-ended question started with one of the five W's and one H, which in journalism is the who, what, when, where, why and the how. Supposedly utilizing these words requires someone to answer a question like this with more than a one word answer.

So, what is the closed-ended question? Questions that start with is, was, could, should or have. For example, I might say to someone, "Would you like a bathroom like this?" It's very easy for them to say yes or no, but it doesn't give me any information. So along the way, somebody got really smart in training and said, "Well, if we use the five Ws and the H from journalism, who, what, when, where, why, how, we'll get more information?" If any of you have ever taken a journalism class you learn that the five W's and one H were established so that a journalist would say, "I need to answer these five Ws and this one H in the first paragraph of my articles, so a person will decide whether or not they want to read the rest of what I've written." So, remember, "Who did this? What did they do? When did they do it? Why did they do it? How did they do it? Where did they do it?" is what the journalist is trying to write about in the first paragraph of their article so that you will have a pretty good idea of what the story's about.

Now, it's not what journalists were taught if they were to become great interviewers. Take a look at Barbara Walters. I'm sure you can find her on YouTube videos. She was one of the greats in creating Socratic questions. Her questions require the person she interviewed to get more than a yes or no answer, and really guided them in a way that helped them be very informative.

Now, when I say a Socratic question, some of you are going to be smart and say, "Deb, it's really not Socratic. It's really not a question per se. Now it's declarative. It's asking somebody to tell you something." True, but let's look at what that does for us in the sales presentation.

Let's use an example. Say your prospect goes into the house. They look at a bedroom, and they say, "I really don't like the look of this room." Now, most of us usually will say, "Why do you feel that way?"

First off, don't start the question with "Why." It comes off with an antagonistic tone as if you're trying to make the prospect feel that she needs to defend what she said. So instead I would say to them, "Tell me some of the reasons that you don't like this room." They can't answer that with a yes or a no. They have to expand on what they said, giving you a more in-depth understanding as to why they don't like the room in general.

Now, why am I going to this length to describe the way I want to be curious and the way that I want to find out more from the prospect? Well, as we'll talk about in a moment, what you're going to learn is the more you know, the easier it is to lead the prospect to an answer. We will talk about this more momentarily because getting them to the answer is more important than you giving them the answer. A great way to start a question is to use the declarative description. Let's use the same example. Again, "I don't like this bedroom." You might say, "Describe some of the things that you don't like about this bedroom." Now I have to use more than one word. I can't just say the color. And even if they did say the color, you can say, "Well, tell me some of the things about the color that really don't gel for you." Do you see, I can continue to use these questions over and over again, to get more and more information. Another way to start a Socratic question is to use the word, "explain."

So, for the same example, the prospect doesn't like the look of the bedroom. You can say, "Explain to me some of the things that you don't like about this bedroom." Okay. Now again, I'm making them give me more information. Another starter is, "Help me understand." You could say, "Help me understand some of the things that you don't like about this room." Or "Help me understand the reasons you feel that way." Again, this requires the prospect to give me more information. Let's use, "Give me an example." I can say in this situation, "Give me an example of one or two things you don't like about this room." Again, I get an explanation. So, if you're always being curious and you are still utilizing Socratic questions that allow you to get more information from someone, you'll always have a better way to help them resolve their concern and create a solution.

Also, when the prospect tells you they don't like something, you should always keep top of mind they are comparing this to something else. They have a vision of something, a reference point. Therefore, you have to find out what this "something they don't like" is being compared to.

When trying to determine the comparison, stay away from, "Compared to what?" That's too blunt, too direct. And again, kind of assertive and really kind of pushy. If I say to them, "Compare this room to something else that you've seen that you like." Now I get the description of the room that they liked. Now I can see where in their comparison, we've not met the expectation. If you don't understand what you're being compared to, then you can never succeed in helping the person resolve the question or objection, it's not possible. You can try, but you won't be successful.

Now in many sales training programs that I've been through, I was always told, think about all the questions and objections someone could have about your product and then create answers. Well, you know, 40 years ago that may have worked. People may have liked that from a sales professional, but now if you have a patented response that people feel has been thought out in advance, that you just pull off the back burner and give to someone, they feel like you're just selling. They feel like you're just pushing them into buying something they don't need, want or desire in today's world. People want to feel special. I don't know how many times you've probably heard this, and I've heard it many times as well. People want to buy; they don't want to be sold. So, if I'm going along and just giving an answer that I've already developed in my head, it sounds like I've boiler plated this, and given this to 25 people ahead of them, they begin to distrust me.

In addition, if the answer to the objection or question sounds very rehearsed, it also makes the buyer think, "I'm not the only person that had this problem. Others probably have this problem. So maybe this is a deficiency in their product." Think about it. A lot of times we come up with this great solution only to forget about the unintended consequences that we may be creating. That creates a problem for us. So again, we need to understand what solutions the buyer can come up with.

Okay, let's just contemplate that for a minute. You want the buyer to think of their own solutions? Yes. So, for those of you who are reading this book who have been in sales for a while, I'm going to use this example. How many times have you been working with a husband and a wife? Let's say, they get into an argument in front of you about something in a home they're considering, and what do we all think? "I'm not getting in the middle of that. I'm going to sit on the sidelines, and I will let them hash it out themselves."

Well, it may be uncomfortable for us, but we've learned that once they hash it out and they come to a solution, that problem is not going to come up again. Well, here is an interesting thought about this. If you come up with a solution and people don't accept it, it will become an objection later when you're trying to close. And what we don't want to have happen is these questions or objections rearing their ugly head later on in the sale. Now it's too late to really create a value statement.

So, what I want to do after I've asked the Socratic question? Let's use our same example, "I don't like this room."

I say, "Well, describe some of the things that you don't like about this room."

And my prospective buyer says, "Well, I just don't think this wall space is going to accommodate my furniture. I just don't really like the way I think I'm going to have to set up my furniture."

Instead of saying, "Well, what furniture do you have?" They tell you and then you say, "Well, let's put the bed over here. Let's put the dresser over here. Doesn't that work?" That's your solution. They want to solve it. The reason they're asking or creating this objection is they're trying to figure this out. This is not a bad thing. This is a good thing. So, what I would say to them is, "Okay. So, you feel like your furniture is not going to fit in this room the way you would like it to, am I right" That's a yes or no question. And that's okay to ask that is a closed-ended question.

They respond, "You're right. That's how I feel." You then respond by saying, " All right, let's do this. Why don't you describe some of the solutions we could potentially use for furnishing this room?" Wow, "I hadn't thought about that." That's what you're usually going to get from the prospect. And now we start working together to see if there are other solutions.

Perhaps the buyer in this situation says, "I was going to put my bed on this wall, but now that I look at it, I could probably put my bed on this wall, but what would I do with the rest of my furniture?" And you say, "You could put your furniture over here. You could do this with your dresser. How would it feel to you now?" Yes. This is a how question? I'm not asking a Socratic question. I really want to know how it would feel if the room was set up this way? The buyer might say, "Well, it would feel great." Okay. So, did we solve the room objection? It didn't feel great because they didn't think that their furniture would fit the way they wanted to set it up. Now we've worked through a solution. They've found the answers to the objection and now they say, "Yes, it would feel great."

Now I do something that's very counterintuitive. Once they say, "Yes, it would be great. This would work." I need to go ahead and ask them one more question. Wait for it… "Is there anything else you don't like about this room?" Why would I ask that question? You're probably thinking I just got them to solve the problem. Now I can go onto something else. Nope. What you need to do is make sure there's nothing else about that room that is a problem for them. Because if you don't ask the question, you're going to get faced with it later. Let's explore all options. Let's talk about all solutions. Let's flush out anything and everything these people could possibly think is a problem about that room before we ever leave the room.

Now, for those of you that are in new home sales, this is very, very important to think about. Let's say you're showing somebody an inventory home. As we go through this process we get them back to our sales office and we start talking about contracting for the home, and they say, "You know, I'm not sure that bedroom was as good as the bedroom at the home that you showed me." You suggest you all go back to look at that home and the buyer says they are out of time. Guess what? You can't go any further. You're at a stall. Sometimes this happens this way because they are planning the stall because they're not sure about whether or not they should move forward. But, in this example you put yourself in that position. When you put yourself in a position where you can't go back and look at something else, you can't go back to that moment in time and say, is there anything else now that they've created other objections.

Now we're hopeful that we can get another appointment and bring them back. This is why it's so very important to solve the problem when it occurs and not later. For those of you who are realtors, imagine this, when you have to show somebody a home and then you haven't resolved all the questions and objections, you take them and show them another home. And then they say, "I think I liked the bedroom at the first home better, but I'm not quite sure that that bedroom really suited my furniture." Now you don't even have the window of being able to go back and show that home today, because you had an appointment time and that's expired. So now we have to either try to get another appointment right then and there, which may or may not be possible or we have to wait until another day. We have just prolonged the process even more. And now when we send these buyers home, they can come up with more objections and more questions and it slows the entire sales process down.

My point to you is even though it feels very counterintuitive to ask for another objection, the more you ask the better your chances are that you're going to flush out every objection they have about that house. The more objections you flush you finally reach a point where no more objections exist. Then you know that you're at a place where you can start to wrap up all the loose ends and actually get to a point where we can put people on contract. Without that, something is always going to rear its ugly head. If you don't resolve everything, I guarantee you that it will always come back to bite you.

ACTION STEPS:

- Take all of the questions that you usually ask people in your sales process. Write those questions down. If they start with who, what, when, where, why or how, or it starts out with any closed ended statements like could, would, should, rewrite those questions in a way that starts with a Socratic question. Rewrite that question to say, "Help me understand, describe to me, give me an example." Any of those will work. So what this does for you, instead of having to learn a whole new process of questioning, it allows you to take the questions you're already comfortable with and to put them in a format that will get you better answers.

- Throw out all of your pre-written answers to people's objections. The more boilerplate, it sounds the less likely the buyer is to accept it. The less likely they are to accept it means the less they trust you. The less they trust you, the less they're likely to buy from you.

- Make sure that you avoid the question, "Why?" Take it out of your vocabulary? Don't require people to defend your positions. If you'll try these three steps this week, and in your sales presentation, you're going to get a much different result.

CHAPTER EIGHT

If You're Closing, You Are Losing

I THOUGHT ABOUT WHAT the title should be for this chapter, and I realize everyone wants to know about closing. People should know that if they're closing they are losing. Interestingly enough, as I thought about this, I'm sure some of you who picked this book up, immediately turned to this chapter because someone has told you that if you're not selling enough, you're not closing hard enough. Well, whoever told you that is so wrong, it's not funny. The harder you close, the less likely you will make a sale! While thinking about this topic I was just looking at my own books that I read. I've got no fewer than ten books on my shelf here that talk about closing. Of course, I have over 75 different books on sales, and every one of them has a chapter on closing. If you go to Amazon, I did that this morning, Amazon has over 148 different books written on closing. If you search Google on how to close a sale, there's one that says there are 25+ workable phrases to do it. Another Google site has 30+ closing tips and techniques to make the sale.

At the very beginning of this book, we talked about some significant things called decision questions, and the premise is that that buyer has to, in their own mind, have found answers or discussed with the salesperson or researched on their own many of these topics. If you remember, "Why would I want to buy this brand?" if I'm buying from a builder or "Why would I want to work with this salesperson or realtor?" Or "Why would I want to buy in this neighborhood?" Remember all those questions? If we're at a point where someone is ready to buy, they have answers, and have come to grips with how that all works for them based on all of those different questions we discussed we are probably at a point where they are ready to buy. However, many, many years ago, when I took sales training classes, I was told that if the buyer has to ask you to buy, you've gone too far. I would submit to you in today's world, the best close is for the buyer to ask you, "What's the next step?" Now not everybody gets there. And so, as a result, we have to have a strategy to be able to wrap this entire process up. And I hate to call it a close because it is not a close. It is really a search for information. Did we get a lot of information? Certainly, we did.

If you go to the old sales training manuals, I guess what you would say is the most effective close out there is what we used to call the summary close. I'm just going to assume they're going to buy based on those strategies and processes we've outlined in the previous chapters. If we've done all that right, and we've answered all the questions a prospect could have, we've delved into the objections and helped them find solutions to their problems. We should probably be at a place where we could safely assume that maybe they're ready to go ahead and buy.

Most people are petrified of asking any sort of closing question because they're afraid of rejection. They're afraid that after all these hours and after all the time and energy they've invested that someone might actually look at them and say, "No, I don't want what you have now." Let's think about that. Let's say you're a new home sales professional, and you've met with this person three, four, or five times and every meeting is somewhere between 30 minutes and two hours and that person's come back that many times. You spent that much energy with them, and they've become that emotionally involved with your product. You really think you're going to say "No?"

Let's say you're one of my realtor friends and you've been out working with this person. You've shown them a multitude of different homes. You've done research online. They've done research online. You've been together working through this process for a couple of weeks. Do you really think they're going to tell you, "No, I don't want to buy a home from you." Probably not. Why do we get so nervous about trying to tie up all these loose ends to put this person on contract? Because at the bottom of our soul, we recognize that when we're trying to ask this closing question, we know there are things left uncovered. We know that we don't know all there is to know about what this buyer is thinking. That's why we're so hesitant. What if I can show you a way that takes all of the guesswork out of it, it takes all the pressure and stress out of it for you and the prospective buyer? What if there were a way to accomplish that? Would that be worthy of knowing? Absolutely it would. I'm sure you're wondering, "Why haven't you already told me?" Well, let's just step back for a moment and think about a few other things.

If the buyer has answered all of these decision questions in their head, they will probably ask you what's our next step. I know what I need to know. I'm ready to move forward. That's a good thing. That means they feel comfortable with the solutions they have, and you can feel comfortable too.

A summary close is always the most effective close because it allows you to refresh your memory and the buyer's memory. Let's walk through what that exactly looks like. When we're ready to move forward, what we want to do is to go back through all of those questions. We know a buyer needs to have answered these questions, and we need to make sure we know their answers.

I'll give you an example. I've worked with somebody for some time. They found a home that they love in a specific neighborhood that works for their family. They haven't said to me yet "What's our next step?" And I realize we're at a place where I need to ask them to move forward. This is the way the summary close goes. "Mr. And Mrs. Smith, we've talked about a lot of things over the five different appointments that we've had together. And I just really want to go through and do a mental checklist to make sure that I've covered everything I need to tell you to help you come up with the best decision. We've had a long conversation about why you believe XYZ home is the type of home you would want to put your family in. You told me that you really like the attention to detail. You felt that this builder's reputation was essential to you. You were impressed by the fact that they have been in the business for 57 years and that their consumer ratings are so high. Am I right?"

Notice that during the closing, I'm only going to ask for a yes or no. I don't need the prospect to go ahead and give me more information. I'm asking them, do they know absolutely what they're getting into?

"We also talked about why you would want to buy this particular home versus the home you already live in now. You described your current home as small. The bedrooms that you currently have don't allow any workspace for your children. There's no room for a desk. Having that room is very important. You mentioned that. You also talked about the need for an open kitchen/ breakfast/ family area so that when your family comes over, everyone feels like they're a part of the party."

You see where I'm going with this. We can go through every part of the home and compare it to the home they currently have.

"So, based on everything that we've talked about, this particular home is a much better fit than the one you already live in, correct?"

"Yes, you're right."

"All right. Mr. and Mrs. Smith, we also talked about the fact that you have looked at some other builder's homes and some of the things you described about my home that you felt were a better fit. What was number one? The amenities that I offer are much more inclusive than the others offered to you. You also talked about the fact that this floor plan's flow is much more conducive to the way your family lives. You liked the ceiling heights in my home which is very important to you."

So technically, we're just going to go on and mention the things that our buyers liked about our model.

"So, based on everything that we've talked about, Mr. and Mrs. Smith, I think that XYZ Homes is a better fit for you, correct? We also looked at the other floor plans that my company offers. We are considering 3 different plans. A, B and C. You told me you like Plan C better because it has a larger kitchen with more storage. It has also a wider entry way than that of Plan A or B. Plan C also fulfills more of the storage needs that you and your husband have than the other two."

Again, you see where I'm going with this? I go through with them everything that makes Plan C a better fit for them as compared to the other two plans.

"So, based on everything that you told me, Mr. and Mrs. Smith, we then agree that plan C is the optimal choice for you with XYZ homes."

"Let's talk a little bit about the area of town that we're in. You told me that you really liked this area of town because it is close to your parents. You have spent a lot of time with them, and often, they babysit your children. This is only a 10-minute drive time, great to drop the kids off. And it's great for them to stop by and see you."

"You also talked about the fact that shopping was very important to you. We have a grocery store just around the corner, a pharmacy two blocks away, and a mall just a half a mile down the street. These are some of the things that you told me made this area optimal for you. Am I right, Mr. and Mrs. Smith?"

"Let's also talk a bit more about this particular neighborhood. It is a gated community. You felt that it was a safer environment for you and your children. You also discussed the fact that you wanted your children to have friends within the neighborhood. We have several families in the neighborhood with children of the same age group that would allow them to create those friendships. So, based on everything we've discussed, Mr. and Mrs. Smith, this neighborhood is a fit for you, right?"

"I also want to talk about the specific lot this house is on. One of the things you told me was important is to have a space for the dogs. Of course, we talked about how this side yard would be a perfect space for them. You were even talking about building a kennel there so that you could leave them outside during the day when the weather's beautiful and you can give them some exercise. We also talked about the need for an area for a trampoline for your children. And we agreed that on this particular lot, this corner would be perfect for that. We also discussed the idea that you like to do a lot of outdoor entertaining, so the spot is fabulous for that because it has an East facing backyard. So, you get the sun in the morning, but not in the afternoon, and you like that."

As you can see, I've gone through a litany of these questions, and I've reiterated to Mr. and Mrs. Smith, all the things they told me were positive about each one of these specific areas. That's why it's so important to remember that these questions are going through people's heads and have to be answered before the buyer is in a position to move forward. So, once I've wrapped all of this up, then this is where I then make the following assumption.

"Based on everything you've just told me, I would like to recommend that we now sit down and get all of this on paper so we can tie up the house and the pricing, and then we can get you with our loan officer and set an appointment with our decorator center."

I never asked them, "So do you want to make this yours? Is this the home for you?" For me, those kinds of questions wouldn't work in closing the deal. There's nothing wrong with asking those questions if that works for you, but for many of us, it won't.

There are also times when we run through the whole summary process that we hit a snag. Take, for example, I was telling Mr. and Mrs. Smith about the backyard and how fitting it is for outdoor activities, then suddenly they have an objection.

They might say, "Actually we said we wanted all that stuff, but now we're not exactly sure that we want an Eastern facing backyard. I mean, I don't know what I really want. In the fall and the spring, when it's getting colder at night, without that sun my back patio might feel too cold when we are entertaining. You know, maybe that's not the best facing backyard."

See, I still haven't asked them to buy. I can stop right there, and say, "Oh gosh, okay. So, there are concerns. Let's talk about that some more." You see, I never had to put myself in a place of rejection ever. That is the beauty of asking people to go through the process with you. You go through your checklist to make sure that you've helped them answer all their questions. It gets them to remember that they said yes to all these questions. Now if you've been through sales training where they say, "Get the yes momentum going," this is the momentum. Every time I ask them a question and they give me a yes, I've got momentum.

The checklist process also helps you determine if you missed something or you inadequately answered one of the buyer's questions. During the process, you can go back to that and discuss the situation with the buyer a little bit more. I just want to make sure we've hit everything. I just want to make sure we've addressed everything. Before I put myself in the rejection seat, before somebody tells me, "No, we don't want to move," I can go back and resolve the issues keeping them from saying yes. And then I can go ahead and affirm that. Either we've stayed on the same lot, or found a different one, I can continue to move forward. Now, if I get all the way to the end and I asked the question, "Based on everything you've told me, then what I would suggest we do is to go back and let's get this all on paper. Let's wrap up all the loose ends. We'll tie up the lot. We'll tie up the pricing," and suddenly they go, "Oh no, no, no, no. We're not ready for that." Now what do you do?

By this time, you still haven't asked them to buy from you. It's perfect because now you can, in all honesty, say, "Gosh, I am so sorry. I would have never recommended us to get to this point of getting the paperwork done if I had known that there was something still not answered on your side. If you still have more questions, please share them with me." That was the Socratic piece I put in there. "Share it with me."

When somebody tells you, "They have to think about it," one of those decision questions still hasn't been answered. So, you talk to the prospects a little bit more. Get them the information they need. Don't be too aggressive and say, "Are you ready to move forward with this today? Are you ready to put your name on the title? Are you prepared to buy this house today; put your name on the dotted line." I've done none of those things. All I did was to summarize everything that they told me.

Finally, if all of those answers have met the buyer's specific needs, then yes, the next natural step in this process is to get all of the paperwork resolved. Notice I said "paperwork," not contract. I've carried that with me all the years that I've been in this business.

Somebody taught me that when I was starting my career in sales, and I think it's still appropriate today. Nobody really wants to sign a contract, but no one really feels too bad about filling out paperwork. I know it's silly, but that's exactly how people feel. So, notice we haven't asked them to buy or asked them about where we are in the process. We suggested the next steps.

In sales, I have seen so many sales professionals asking their prospects to buy the house today. And we're always talking in business about creating urgency. The reason they're not buying today is I haven't created urgency. Well, from a psychological standpoint, urgency cannot be created. External urgency is like motivation. And in psychology, when we're working with people, we realize that people's motivation is an internal construct, not an external construct. What does that mean? Well, if I'm motivated to do something, it comes from within so no matter how much people might pressure me to do something, I only do it if I really want to do it. Same thing with urgency, you cannot push people into buying something.

If you do and are successful in the push, here's what usually happens. The next day, you're going to get a call saying they want to cancel that contract because they felt pushed or prodded or they didn't know what else to do to get away from you.

I want to tell you a story about this guy, Tom, who I worked with many years ago. Tom was a fascinating guy. He was fast-talking and fast-moving. He kept you on the edge of your seat because you never knew what was going to happen next. Tom would get in front of prospects, and he would start working with them. He would dazzle them with his brilliance. He was very smart about his product; he always gives his prospects alternative choices.

Choices. "Would you like this or this?" Or "Do you want to do this or this?" And he kept getting people to answer all of these. Yes or no questions. And there are people in the world who say that if you can get people to agree to an alternative choice, you make them make more little decisions. So, when it comes time to make the big decision, they move forward. Well, I don't know, maybe that worked in 1962, but I don't see that working very effectively in this era. Why? Because people have become very smart shoppers. In 1965, they didn't have the resources they have today. They didn't have the internet. They didn't have all the knowledge they have today. And so, a lot of times you could do things many, many years ago that you certainly would never be able to get away with today.

So back to Tom. He was a fun guy. If you went to a sales presentation with him, it was fun. He would work with these people for a couple of hours. He would keep them until I could tell you that they looked dog tired when they walked back to the sales office. He had kept them going for two hours, and then he would ask them to close, "Let's go ahead and make this yours." And they would sign. In fact, one year when I worked with Tom, he had 63 people who actually said yes and signed. Do you want to know how many people he actually closed? You will be shocked. I was shocked. Only 9 of them actually made it to closing. How do you write 63 contracts and have everyone but nine cancel out?

Well, I actually started doing some research on it, and you know what? We found out a lot of people were so dazzled by Tom, and they were so caught up in the presentation that they just got caught up in the moment. And when they got home, or they were driving home, they asked, "What did we just do earlier? I didn't want to buy that house. It was just so much fun. I didn't know what to do." That was about 40% of the people he worked with. The other 60% that I talked to said they felt so pressured, like they couldn't get away from Tom. He just kept them hamstrung. And to get away from him, they said yes, knowing that they could call the next day and say no and cancel payment on their checks.

So, the question becomes, how does somebody who can write 63 contracts only get 9 of them to close? Was Tom a great closer? I can tell you a lot of people thought he was, but the results tell you otherwise. What is the point of closing on someone if they never actually close on the house? That's a lot of time and money lost and a lot of energy wasted. Imagine how devastated Tom was thinking he was the number one producer for that company that year because he had written 63 sales. He wasn't, he was at the bottom of the ranks because only nine of them stuck. Don't pressure people. Don't press them to do what you want them to do. Don't sit there with them for hours on hours and hours that they will get so tired that they finally say, "Yes." But all that's going to result in is a cancellation tomorrow.

You cannot create external urgency and make it work. What is external urgency? My favorite, especially with home builders, is to tell potential buyers the price will go up. You don't want to pay more money than you need to for home. Most people call them to say, "I want to let you know, prices are going up. Don't miss out." Guess what? They usually respond, "I'm not going to buy a home over $2,000 or $3,000. I'm going to buy what I want to buy. And you're not going to force me to move any faster than I'm going to move." This almost feels like you are giving them an incentive to buy.

Remember, incentives are something you truly offer an individual to get them to do something they might otherwise not do. Now you normally might offer incentives to children that maybe weren't doing all that well in school. Parents would say, "If you get 's, we'll do this," right? That's an incentive because you felt like your children would never get the A unless you put the carrot out there for better results. But it usually doesn't work. It backfires on you. And the more you try to pressure people externally, by telling them they need to buy before prices go up, or they're going to lose that lot, or they need to buy because someone else is going to build the same plan across the street, you just never make the sale.

Now, obviously we go through markets where perhaps there are people all trying to buy the same home. Guess what? People know that. People also read that in the news. For example, if you're one of my realtor friends, maybe you've had a client thinking about putting an offer in on a house or home and they wait two days and then they find out it's already been sold to somebody else. All you need is to have a buyer lose out on a home because they waited too long. I guarantee you, you won't have to worry about creating any urgency. Let's make sure we do the right thing with people. Make sure we truly understand what it is they want and need. And then let's make sure that we have helped them go through in their mind that we have gotten what they need by answering all these questions and go through everything else that they need to know before they buy.

Let's talk about three things we most often hear. These are some of the ways that you can handle the most frequently heard reasons for not moving forward. Number one, "I have to think about it." Don't be combative. If they have to think about it, here's what I do. I actually apologize. What? Why am I apologizing? This is what I would say. I would say to the person, "I am so sorry that I've spent this much time with you and there are still things you have left to think about. Obviously, I've not done the best in answering all your questions. What have I missed?" Or if I'm using my Socratic questions, "Tell me some of the things you are still thinking about that I really didn't explain fully for you."

Now, you may still get the person that says to you, "I'm going to have to think about it because that's what my husband and I do. We always go home and talk about it before we make the final determination." I'm just going to tell you if that's their rule, you're probably not going to break the rule.

I've been taught along the way to say things like, "Well, if this works tomorrow and you had to give me your answer, what do you think your answer might be?" I don't think that's really very effective these days. Please respect people's needs to think about it if that's their plan of action.

If I've done really well in creating a great sales strategy, somewhere in my process, I will have asked them what decision-making process they will go through in making the decision on what to buy. If I understand that, then I shouldn't be shocked and amazed when this comes up if I try to close. I'm not going to say, "Let's go to the next step," if they had told me in the process that every time they buy anything of this magnitude they get all the information, look through it and then go home to talk before making a decision. My recommendation is not going to be to move ahead and get all the paperwork put together. My process is now going to be based on what they told me before. They're going to want to go home and have that conversation. So I know that's what they need to do.

Now in giving them that time I might say, "How much time do you think you'll need? And let's go ahead and set a time to get back together." Let's say they say they need 24 hours. I would suggest, "Let's get back together tomorrow at two o'clock and let's have a conversation about any other questions that may have arisen." Notice, I didn't say anything about getting the paperwork done, only "Let's get back together." People don't want to be pressured. I can't say that enough. So again, I saved myself the anxiety. I saved myself from the rejection. If I know the processes they need to go through in making their decision, then let's let them go through that. People are more likely to come back to you and say, "Sure, we'd be happy to chat with you," because they don't feel like the next step is you forcing them to buy a home.

Number two. "We need to explore all of our options." Again, I am going to respond in the same way, "I am so sorry. I've obviously missed something. I thought that we had found the right home on the right block in the right neighborhood, in the right area. The fact that you still feel you need to explore some options says I was incorrect, that you don't feel this is the best solution. Let's talk about some of the reasons you don't feel this is the best solution for you." You see, I'm not calling them out on the carpet. I'm not questioning why they feel a certain way. I am asking them to give me more information. Which, by the way is really true, if they're still not ready to move forward, then you obviously have missed something, and you do owe them an apology. And what if you have the ultimate of all ultimate's, "If it's gone when we come back, it wasn't meant to be." Really? To me, that means this person is nowhere close to buying.

Interestingly enough, that comes up frequently when we make one major mistake. What is it? Closing too early. And you're probably wondering what exactly closing too early means. Well, what I've learned in working with prospects and sales professionals in today's world is when a prospect starts to ask questions, for example, "What earnest money is required if we went on contract and how long would it take to get the home? What title company would we need to use?" All of those questions were taught to us many years ago as buying questions, right? It's a signal they're making buying decisions.

I hate to tell you that's not true anymore. Those are just questions. Buyers are much more educated today. They've gone online and they started researching how to buy a home. They know earnest money is going to be required. It's a natural question about how much they need to buy a home with you and doesn't necessarily mean they want to buy the home that you just showed them. All they're saying is I know earnest money is going to be required.

When you start taking some of these questions that people ask, like the ones I've just given you and you think those are buying signs, then you start to close too early. And when you close too early, all the questions have not been answered. You start to jump to the end of the line way too quickly. That's when you start to get these weird responses, like, "If it's meant to be, it'll be here tomorrow." Most people that have gone through the process, don't feel that way. They're trying to make a rational decision and feel comfortable with where they're going.

If a sales professional is getting a lot of these types of questions I always ask, "How long were you with this person before you asked the closing question?" And usually when these things blow up, they've only been with somebody 45 minutes or an hour. I've worked with builders who send in mystery shoppers to go through the sales process to gauge how effective it is. They have video taken and about 98% of the salespeople are asking that shopper to commit to buying a home within 45 to 50 minutes because the shopper's given them a lot of positives. They feel like there's momentum going. And they just assume that now's the time to ask. Every time the shopper says, "Well, we need to think about it." I'll tell you, if you're asking someone that you're working with to buy a home in 45 minutes or less, it's not a sale.

In fact, I've only sold a house once in less than 45 minutes in my entire career, and it was a unique situation. I had a baseball player moving into town. He was there with his wife who was nine plus months pregnant. She was having labor pains while they were looking at this home with me. I can assure you, we got that decision made in 45 minutes or less, and she was in the labor room that night and delivered a baby four hours after they left my office. That's the only time that that's happened to me in my career.

Now maybe some of you may be lucky and it's happening more frequently. But most of the people that I talked to have told me the same thing, that when they're asking somebody to buy in 45 minutes or less, it's not a sale. So if you've spent a short period of time with these people and just because they seem like they liked what you had, or you got a lot of yes momentum going and you decided to just go for the kill, you're probably not going to get the answer that you want.

So remember if you're closing, if you're actually asking somebody to make it theirs or to put their name down on the paperwork in that short period of time, then you're probably losing more than you're winning.

However, if you'll go through the process of making sure that you have, in fact, helped that prospect or buyer answer all those questions and they have to have answers they need before they feel comfortable making the buying decision your buyer is in a very different position. When you get all those yeses because you've answered their questions, it's just a logical conclusion that the very next step would be to get all the paperwork out of the way to make it theirs. It's that simple.

ACTION STEPS:

- Think about the kind of close you use. Is that a pressure tactic or is it actually a summary that helps somebody understand all the questions they had? And make sure you have answers for all of them. If you're not summarizing all the things you've discussed and making sure they're in agreement, then you're probably losing more than you're winning.

- Closing is never an event. Just like negotiation, it's a process. If I'm finding out all the appropriate information along the way, then it should culminate in a natural conclusion that says, this is the home I want to buy.

- Don't worry about rejection. If, in fact, somebody says to you they're not ready, then always apologize. Because in truth, you owe them an apology for taking that much time and not getting them any closer to the ultimate thing they really want. And that's to be put in a position to buy the home of their dreams.

Conclusion

FIRST OFF, LET ME thank you for getting all the way through this book. Not all of it was easy. Not all of it was something that you probably immediately believed in. Most people think they get into sales because they have the gift of gab, but it isn't about who knows how to talk the most, it's about who asks the best questions. It's about who understands their buyer better than anyone else. And it's about who helps that buyer find the right solutions to their problems. Selling is not really a fly by the seat of your pants career if you want to be super successful at it. Selling is also not something you're just born with. I've heard so many times you have to be a natural at it. No, you don't. I've seen lots and lots of people that when you met them on the street, you would have never thought they would have been super successful in selling. Yet they are.

Selling is a strategy and a process. If you follow that process and that strategy with every person, your success ratio is going to become greater and greater. The reason most people lose a sale is they didn't follow the process. The reason they lost the sale is because they didn't understand their buyer. They really didn't know what they needed, or they talked too much. This particular outline gives you a strategy and a process to use.

Every time you meet a customer, one thing you'll want to do is start to deviate. My answer to you is don't it, just say no. When you deviate from the process and the strategy and start making it up on the fly, things start to fall apart. Many of you may have picked up this book because you just want to become a better sales professional. Still, I'm going to guess most of you who picked up this book, don't feel like your sales numbers reflect what you want to accomplish in this business.

If you're not selling, and you're not hitting the numbers that you want to hit, go back to the beginning and figure out what you're missing. I guarantee you something in one of the previous chapters is exactly the key to unlock the success you want. I can guarantee you that if you follow this process, you can maximize your opportunities for success in sales. Why would I make that kind of guarantee? Because I've seen this work time and time again, I've seen it work for professionals who have done this for 15, 20 years, who decided that maybe they didn't know everything they thought they did, so they're ready to try a new way. And I've watched people who had almost no sales experience employ these strategies and tactics and become superstars, passing up the people who had been the old pros in no time flat.

I will give you a final couple of examples. Jane was working for one of the builders I was involved with. And Jane went to a neighborhood that she really didn't want to go to, but her boss had asked her to go there. She didn't feel like she really fit in with the people that were buying there. She didn't feel there was a match and she complained and complained about how horrible it was and how much time she was there with very little result. I said to Jane, "Look at your process. Are you following the process? Are you following this strategy? Are we just winging it every day?"

And because we had a great relationship, she looked at me and said, "You know what? I've just been winging it. I promise you I'll follow the process." Her sales rate went from two a month to 15 the very next month. Why? She changed her strategy. She utilized the process.

I have another person I've worked with who graduated from college and went into selling for this builder. He actually started as an assistant to another sales professional, and he worked very, very hard. And James, we'll call him, had wanted to become a sales professional, and soon he got his chance. This company put him in a close-out community. If you've worked in this business at all, you know, when it's closeout, 9 times out of 10, you can't even sell your model floor plan anymore because it's sold out. You can only build certain homes on certain lots because that's all that fits, and you don't have any of those other options to show anyone.

James told me, "I can't show the model. I can't utilize my model. I can't sell it."

And I told him, "You know, that'll be the best experience you've ever had. Let's stick with the process. It's not worrying about whether or not we have a model that we can show. Let's demonstrate the model like we talked about. Let's talk about features of how a home lives. People like to look at how they will utilize their home. How do they envision utilizing this space? Let's use that. And I guarantee you we'll find some plans they can fit into." He agreed and went through that process. He sold out of that neighborhood that only had 10 opportunities left in just two months.

He then took on a neighborhood that one of the old professionals called, "A deal that will never work. There's no way that's going to be a home run." Well, this young man went into that community, took it on and sold it out in less than a year, and became one of the top-selling sales professionals in that company. He'd only had basically six months of experience before he got into that situation, and he sold more homes than sales professionals who had been doing the job for over 20 years.

The process works. The question is, are you willing to change where you are and what you're currently doing? Suppose you're somebody that's been doing this for 15 or 20 years, and you view yourself as the ultimate professional. In that case, my question is, are you willing to change? Are you willing to try something new? Are you willing to take the things that you already do that are part of this strategy and augment them with other pieces that you've never utilized? Or are you going to be somebody who resists change and says, "There's nothing more for me to learn."

You might've been the person who just skipped immediately to Chapter Eight and said, "Evidently, I'm not closing hard enough. I need a new closing tool." And then you were sorely disappointed because I didn't give you 135 different ways to close. You need to follow the process. If you commit to taking this on, I know from doing this with so many other sales professionals that you CAN attain results you didn't even believe were possible.

I know all of this works. I know that if you embrace these strategies and make them yours, your level of success and what you want to achieve in this world of sales will be mind-blowing. You will achieve things that you didn't probably even think possible. And to this end, I wish every one of you good luck, much success, and as always, happy selling!

THANK YOU FOR READING MY BOOK!

DOWNLOAD YOUR FREE GIFTS

Read This First

Just to say thanks for buying and reading my book, I would like to give you a 100% bonus gift for FREE, no strings attached!

To Download Now, Visit:
www.NoRoomForFailureBook.com/freegift

I appreciate your interest in my book, and I value your feedback as it helps me improve future versions of this book. I would appreciate it if you could leave your invaluable review on Amazon.com with your feedback. Thank you!

www.ingramcontent.com/pod-product-compliance
Lightning Source LLC
Chambersburg PA
CBHW061042110426
42740CB00050B/2758